Introduction

This purpose of this guide is to provide a quick and easy reference for anyone working in and around the City of Liverpool. We have tried to strike a difficult balance. On the one hand we aim to give clear, accurate information on some of the essential beliefs, practises and customs of people of faith in our City, whilst avoiding over-simplistic generalisations that can re-enforce rather than break down stereotypes. Hence our repeated 'Health warning' towards the end of each chapter.

On the other hand, we wish to keep the guide as accessible to as wide a range of people as possible.

This booklet arose out of Liverpool Community Spirit's work in promoting understanding and practical co-operation between people of diverse faiths and also those who do not adhere to any single major faith tradition. It forms part of our Adult Learners Course on Faith Diversity in Liverpool and is aimed at anyone who is interested in broadening their basic understanding of Liverpool's uniquely rich diversity of faith community heritage.

To start acquiring any genuine understanding of a faith necessarily requires face to face meeting and practical engagement with those individuals from the faith communities who struggle to practise it. This guide will only fulfil our aims if it encourages the reader to meet, open their hearts and engage in honest dialogue with their neighbours from those faith communities that are unfamiliar to them.

The illustrations are taken from the Liverpool Round Table of Faiths. This is a Liverpool Community Spirit project that brought together young people from the City of Liverpool to explore and celebrate our wonderful faith community heritage. A brief explanation is provided in the last chapter.

THE BAHA'I COMMUNITY

Faith: **Baha'i**
Faith Community: **Baha'i**

Holy Books/Scriptures:
The Writings/Scriptures of the three central figures, Bab, Baha'u'llah and Abdu'l Baha

Sacred Languages:
Baha'is do not view one language more sacred than another but the sacred writings are in Persian and Arabic.

Core Belief:
Belief in the Oneness of God, the Oneness of religion and the Oneness of mankind. The central theme of Baha'ullah's (founder of the Baha'i faith) message is **unity**. Baha'is believe in the common foundation of all religions and believe that Baha'u'llah was the latest in a line of **messengers** from God that include Abraham, Krishna, Moses, Zoroaster, the Buddha, Jesus Christ and Muhammad (pbuh). Religion and revelation are seen as progressive and ongoing. Whilst the spiritual message remains eternally the same, the practical teachings and guidance of religion has to **evolve** and progress. The Baha'i faith was particularly forward looking and revolutionary in its stress upon the following core elements of Baha'i belief:

i   The equality of men and women.
ii Universal education.
iii The eradication of poverty wealth and injustice.

Most religious historians believe that the Baha'i faith arose from Shi'ah Islam, similar to the way that Christianity arose out of Judaism. In 1844 Siyyid Ali Muhammad assumed the title '***Bab***' = 'The Gate', explaining that his mission was to herald the arrival of 'One greater than himself' who would fulfil all the prophetic expectations of the great religions of the world. This date is seen as the beginning of the Baha'i faith. His followers were known as Babis and 1000s were slaughtered for their beliefs by the Muslims in Iran. In 1863 one of his followers, Mirza Husayn Ali-I-Nuri, received a message from God whilst imprisoned and realised he was the Manifestation predicted by the Bab and he assumed the title ***Baha'u'llah*** ('The Glory of God').

Baha'is believe that Baha'u'llah is the Messenger of God for this age and the Promised One of all religions. The last 40 years of his life were spent in prison or exile, the last 22 of which were in present day Israel, hence the headquarters of the faith is at Haifa. His eldest son, Abdul-Baha was appointed by his father to be the interpreter of his teachings and the Centre of his covenant. Abdul Baha established the institution called the Guardianship (of the Baha'i faith) and appointed Shoghi Effendi as the Guardian of the Faith after himself.

Baha'is have suffered repeated and widespread persecution from orthodox Muslims, for whom Muhammad is the seal of the Prophets and Messengers. Baha'is point out that the Qur'an says that Muhammad is the seal of the Prophets and not the seal of the Messengers.

Annual events relating to Faith:
Baha'is do not proselytise and are only allowed to talk about their faith when asked/invited to do so.

There are an estimated 6 million followers of the Baha'i faith. The Baha'i era is denoted by the letters B.E. and dates from the declaration of the Bab in Baha'i calendar is made up of nineteen months consisting of nineteen days per month the remaining days are called Intercalary Days (Time for hospitality, charity and giving of gifts).

Event:	Date:	Significance:
Period of Fast	2nd-20th March	Falls in Baha'i month of Ala. Abstain from food and drink from sunrise to sunset. A time of prayer, reflection and spiritual increase. Fasting obligatory for those over age of fifteen. The traveller, those who are weak or ill are not obliged to fast. No-one is obliged to make up days 'lost' through illness etc.
Feast of Naw-Ruz	20th 21st March	Baha'i New Year. Marks the end of the 19th Day fast. Time of celebration.
Feast of Ridvan	21st April-2nd May	Twelve day feast commemorating the Declaration of Baha'ullah's Mission. The most important day in the Baha'i calendar. Baha'is are forbidden to work on the twelfth day.
Anniversary of the Declaration of Bab	23rd May	Celebration of the declaration of the Bab's revelation of his mission to his first disciple Mulla Husayn in 1844. Also coincides with the birthday of Abdu'l-Baha.
Anniversary of the Ascension of Baha'u'llah	29th May	Commemorating the death Baha'u'llah in 1892. Solemn day of prayer and discussion.
Martyrdom of Bab	9th July	Solemn day of commemorating the death by firing squad of the Bab.
Birth of Bab	20th October	Born in 1819, Persia.
Birth of Baha'u'llah	12th November	Born in 1817, Tehran, Persia.
Day of the Covenant	26th November	Day venerating Abdu'l Baha.
Ascension of Abdul Baha	28th November	Commemorating the ascension of Abdul Baha.

Daily acts of Faith:

Three very short or one very long obligatory prayer can be recited daily for those who have reached age of maturity (15).

Weekly acts of Faith/devotion:

Firesides: Baha'is do not have set worship services or priesthood. Most Baha'i gatherings take place in people's homes, known as Firesides. Baha'is and non-Baha'is can meet and discuss. Meetings would traditionally begin and end with a prayer.

Monthly Acts of Faith/devotion:

The Feast: at the beginning of every Baha'i month, the local community gathers together for the Feast. There are usually three parts to this:
1 Spiritual: prayers and readings then:
2 Consultation: community members discuss and communicate concerns to assembly members, followed by:
3 Social: food and, sometimes, entertainment.

Food:

Generally, there are no specific requirements pertaining to food. Baha'is are not religiously forbidden from eating any particular food. However vegetarianism is commended. Alcohol is forbidden (including its use in cooking) and all drugs (including tobacco) are discouraged.

Greetings:

Allah' u' Abha - 'God is the all Glorious'

Dress:

There are no religious guidelines regarding dress aside from modesty and moderation.

Speech:

Consideration must be shown with regard the use of offensive language or behaviour.

Religious Symbols/Imagery: Baha'is have only a minimal use of symbols and imagery: Pictures of Abdul Baha are quite commonly found in Houses of Worship and Baha'i homes but the only picture of Baha'u'llah is in his shrine and not duplicated.

The Ring Stone or Greatest Name Symbol: this is often worn on a ring or pendant. It is comprised of three horizontal strokes, two stars and a single vertical stroke running through the horizontals. The three horizontal strokes represent the three planes of existence: top = God; central = Manifestations of God (God's prophets), including the two stars = the Bab and Baha'u'llah; lower = humanity.
The vertical line running through and connecting them all = The Holy Spirit. Abdul Baha is thought to have designed it.

Nine-Pointed star: Nine is the numerical value of the name Baha'u'llah in Arabic.

Visiting Place of Worship:
There are seven 'Houses of Worship' across the world. These are continental as opposed to local/national places of worship. However, services are held regularly. The oldest House of Worship is in the United States. They all have nine sides and doors to welcome all major Faiths and a central dome symbolising the diversity and unity of humanity.

Most Baha'i gatherings take place in people's homes.

Baha'is consider Israel to be a particularly Holy Place and it houses the Baha'i Universal House of Justice and the shrines of the Holy Family.

Structure:
Universal House of Justice - in Haifa - is the global governing body. Its nine members are elected by the National Spiritual Assemblies.

National Spiritual Assemblies: supervise national Baha'i communities.

Local Spiritual Assemblies - (where there are more than nine adult believers) administer local Baha'i communities. Each Assembly has nine annually elected members; chair, secretary, treasurer.

Baha'is have no clergy, sacraments or rituals.

Every year, nine people are elected to the Local Assembly to run the affairs of the local Baha'i community. Nine people are elected to run the National Spiritual Assembly and the national Baha'i; community. Nine people from each National Spiritual Assembly are elected onto the Universal Spiritual Assembly.

Gender Issues:
Equality across humanity is paramount. Baha'is stress the equality between men and women. If education is not available to all, then women have priority because they are the educators of the next generation. Women are free to pursue their own careers. Men are expected to help in household duties and childrearing.

Marriage:
Marriage is seen as the basic unit of society, which has to be healthy and unified to ensure the health and unity of society. Monogamous marriage is the foundation of family life. Marriages are not arranged, but parental approval must be sought. Divorce is permitted after one year of 'patience' when counselling and support may be tried.

Death:
Baha'is believe that the body is the temple of the spirit and must be treated with respect and honour. Cremation is forbidden. and the body must not be transported more that one hour away from place of death. The body is shrouded in silk or cotton and a ring bearing a specific inscription is placed on deceased's finger. The body is placed in a coffin made of crystal stone or hard, fine wood.

GENERAL FAITH HEALTH WARNING:

- A little knowledge can be very dangerous! Treat all people of a faith as individuals and beware of generalisations.
- Be aware that there is a great diversity of belief and practise within each faith.
- Ask 'What do you do?' NOT 'Why do you do it?' Don't expect people to know and have to explain/justify WHY they do something.
- Always treat objects held to be sacred with great respect: e.g. holy books, sacred pictures, special items of clothing and jewellery, prayer beads, food and incense that may have a sacred value for the person.

Liverpool's Baha'i Community and Heritage:

Liverpool has a small, but very active and important Baha'i community with a great heritage. The son and successor of Baha'u'llah, Abdu'l Baha, visited Liverpool in 1912, landing in the Albert Dock. Whilst in Liverpool he gave two talks, one at Pembroke Chapel and the other at the Theosophist Society. He stayed at the Adelphi hotel. The numbers of Baha'is grew until, in 1950, there were enough members to elect a Liverpool Local Spiritual Assembly. Baha'is began to meet at the surgery of Dr Ernest Miller in Langdale Rd (he had become a Baha'i). When he died, he kindly left the house to the community. The house next door was bought later and the two were joined to form the Liverpool Baha'i Centre and National Teaching Institute.

Thanks and acknowledgements to:

Nigel Devereux	*Liverpool Baha'i Community (and Liverpool Community Spirit)*
Isaac De Cruz	*Liverpool Baha'i Community*
Denia Kincade	*Liverpool Baha'i Community*

THE BUDDHIST COMMUNITY

Faith: **Buddhism**
Faith Community: **Buddhist**

Holy Books/Scriptures:

After Buddha's death his teachings were collected in three categories called the 'Three Baskets' (Sanskrit: *Tripitaka*). The *Vinaya* is concerned with monastic discipline; the *Sutra* contains the discourses of Buddha and is the basis for Buddhist meditation practice. The *Abhidharma* contains scholastic treatises and primarily focuses on philosophical and psychological topics. Furthermore, there is the collection of Buddhist Tantras, which outline specific meditation practices of the *Vajrayana (Diamond Way)* traditions, mainly practiced within Tibetan Buddhism.

Core Belief:

Buddhists follow the practical teachings of Siddhartha Gautama, the Buddha ('Sakyamuni Buddha'), who lived in India c. 2,500 years ago. **Buddha** is a title which means 'awakened/ enlightened one'.

Buddhism is a very practical faith focusing on the removal of personal suffering and the attainment of joyful and compassionate states of mind. It does not proclaim dogma and encourages critical questioning.

Buddhist teaching is grounded in the practical experience of the Buddha, who is also called '*Tathagata*', meaning 'he who has gone before' (i.e. he is the one who has had the practical experience and travelled the journey of life and liberation before). He explained what exists ultimately and what is conditioned in an immediate way directly relevant to our lives. This understanding makes the experience of lasting happiness possible.

To achieve this goal three poisons, the root cause for all our suffering and frustration in life have to be overcome: **ignorance, attachment** and **aversion**.

The Buddha taught practical methods for eradicating these three poisons and for developing wisdom and compassion.

The methods centre on:

1 Meditation/**Mindfulness** to calm ones mind, see more clearly how cause and effect (*Karma*) works in ones own life and to gain an ultimate insight into the nature of phenomena.
2. Selfless, **compassionate** thoughts and actions.
3 The strengthening of positive states of mind and transformation of negative impressions waiting to mature into wisdom.

Within Buddhism 'Karma' does not mean fate, but rather *cause and effect*. These teachings highlight that all beings are responsible for their own lives. This understanding makes it possible to consciously generate the positive impressions, which bring happiness and help avoid the cause of future suffering.

3 The strengthening of positive states of mind and transformation of negative impressions waiting to mature into **wisdom**.

Within Buddhism 'Karma' does not mean fate, but rather *cause and effect*. These teachings highlight that all beings are responsible for their own lives. This understanding makes it possible to consciously generate the positive impressions, which bring happiness and help avoid the cause of future suffering.

The heart of Buddhism has been expressed in the form of the **Four Noble Truths**. They are:

1 Human life is full of suffering and is unsatisfactory.
2 The cause of suffering is ignorance, which leads to attachment and aversion and negative actions motivated by it.
3 Lasting well-being and happiness can be attained. Since the cause of all suffering lies within our selves, so the cause of its cessation and the attainment of lasting happiness lies within ourselves.
4 There is a way of attaining this lasting happiness. It is known as the Middle Way (between the extremes of self-indulgence and self-destruction). In some Buddhist traditions (especially the *Theravada*) it is explained as the Noble Eightfold Path:

1 right view
2 right intention
3 right speech
4 right actions
5 right livelihood
6 right effort
7 right mindfulness
8 right concentration

All aspects are developed simultaneously in order to achieve enlightenment, the perfected state of mind.

The two most fundamental values of Buddhism are Wisdom (overcoming ignorance) and Compassion for all sentient beings (overcoming self-centredness).

Buddhists have deep trust and confidence or 'take refuge' in the *Three Precious Jewels*.

- *The Buddha*: understood either as the historical teacher or the perfected state of mind and the goal of all Buddhist practice

- *The Dharma*: the teaching, understanding and practical way that he demonstrated

- *The Sangha*: the community of Buddhists who practice the Dharma in this life

Traditionally, most Buddhist branches had a strong emphasis on monasticism although at all times there were much larger numbers of lay practitioners than monks or nuns. Monks and nuns take vows including chastity, non-violence and being free of personal possessions. They are treated with respect by lay people as they are seen as living examples of the Dharma and representing the Sangha. In general, close physical contact with monks and nuns should be avoided, although not all traditions are very strict about it. In Asia it was custom for lay people to provide for all the material needs of the monks/nuns. While this is still the case for some Buddhist Schools in the West, more and more monks/nuns now also are in conventional employment.

Schools/denominations of Buddhism:

Many different schools of Buddhism have evolved over the centuries, each with a different emphasis upon aspects of the Buddha's teaching and methods of seeking enlightenment. These schools can be subdivided in different ways, but the most popular division distinguishes three approaches:

The *Theravada* ('Words of the Elders of the Order') is the dominant tradition in Southeast Asia and is particularly strong in Thailand, Sri Lanka, Burma, Laos and Cambodia. It bases its teachings and practice on the Pali Canon, which it considers to be the only authentic Buddhist canon.

The *Mahayana* ('Greater Way') is prominent in many parts of Northern Asia, including China, Japan (here especially as the various schools of Zen Buddhism), Mongolia, Tibet and Himalayan countries like Bhutan and Nepal. Mahayana emphasises the ideal of the **Bodhisattva**, who strives to reach enlightenment for the benefit of all beings. The two main aspects of practice focus on the development of compassion and wisdom.

The *Vajrayana* ('Diamond Way') is mainly practiced in Himalayan countries, especially in Bhutan and Tibet and it is thus often also referred to as Tibetan Buddhism. Although Vajrayana practices are rooted in the Theravada and Mahayana, they emphasise teachings on the Buddha Nature (the enlightened potential in every sentient being) and employ powerful meditation practices that are supposed to promote swift personal development towards wisdom and compassion. Followers of virtually all the major schools can be found in the UK.

Annual events relating to Faith:

The Buddhist traditions commemorate different events during the year, but most schools (especially Theravada Schools) celebrate Vesak, although the dates may differ between traditions.

Event:	Date:	Significance:
Vesak	Full moon day of the month 'Visaka' (April/May)	Day of birth, enlightenment and 'death of the Buddha
Full moon day Day		Particularly used for meditation - as it is said that birth, enlightenment and death of Buddha occurred on a full moon.

Daily acts of Faith/Devotion:
At home most Buddhists would have a small shrine. A painting or statue of Buddha would be central, and incense, flowers and candles may be placed beside. Buddhists would aim at spending time daily in meditation and - in line with their particular tradition - may also recite particularly important scriptures (e.g. the *Lotus Sutra*) or follow other rituals supporting their confidence and trust in Buddha, Dharma and Sangha.

Weekly acts of Faith:
Many Buddhists will meet together on a weekly basis for meditation, studying the Dharma, providing mutual support and instruction in the application of their practice in everyday life, or perform specific more ritualistic practices.

It is common in most Buddhist traditions for practitioners to visit the nearest meditation centre or a monastery (or '*vihara*') to receive spiritual support, instruction and guidance provided by experienced practitioners. In some traditions monks and nuns mainly fill this role.

In addition, many Buddhists will deepen their spiritual practice by attending residential retreats.

Food:
There are no strict rules. Buddha advised to avoid eating meat from an animal directly killed for being served at a particular occasion and otherwise to eat what is offered. This is interpreted in different ways by different traditions and individuals. Thus, some Buddhists are vegetarian. Those who are not fully vegetarian may eat fish or eggs. Followers of some traditions, however, may eat meat but not fish. If planning an event, it is therefore advisable to inquire in advance about specific dietary requirements.

Greetings:
It is common for Buddhists to follow the customs of the culture they live in. In some formal or monastic settings, Buddhist may greet each other by placing hands together over the chest and bowing to show recognition and respect for the Buddha or enlightened potential within each one of us.

Dress:
There is no particular dress code in Buddhism and dress varies according to customs and national community. When encountering monks or nuns principles of modesty and respect should be observed. Monks and nuns of the Theravada school shave their heads and wear orange or ochre coloured robes, those of the more northern traditions (i.e. Mahayana, and Vajrayana) usually wear dark red or maroon robes.

Speech:
We have seen that 'right speech' belongs to the eight-fold path of Buddhist practice. Thus Buddhists try to refrain from harsh, rude, harmful or untrue speech and seek to promote gentle, courteous, true and compassionate speech.

Religious Symbols/Imagery:
Statues of the Buddha are very common aids to focus attention and assist concentration on the virtues and teaching represented by the image. They may also be seen as a reminder for ones' own inherent potential for spiritual perfection. Images of **Bodhisattvas** (those highly accomplished beings on the path towards enlightenment) are common amongst followers of Mahayana traditions. Buddhism also has a rich heritage of beautiful sacred paintings of Buddhas and Bodhisattvas and also mandalas (specific psychological diagrams used to aid meditation), which are commonly found on walls of monasteries and houses. The most commonly used symbol for the faith itself is the eight-spoked wheel, representing the eight-fold path.

Visiting a Place of Worship:
Apply principles of respect and modesty and feel free to ask if in doubt about certain details. A Centre/Temple/Monastery will display at least one statue of Buddha. Statues should not be touched. The Centre/Temple/Monastery is a place of teaching religious observance and meditation and may have adjacent accommodation for residents who look after the site and may be monks or nuns.

In line with the particular tradition, offering of flowers, food and incense may be taken. When entering a shrine room one should dress modestly and remove shoes. In most Asian traditions pointing towards a person or a shrine with the soles of ones shoes or feet is seen as an offence and should be avoided.

Visiting a Home:
Principles of respect, modesty and cleanliness apply. If in doubt, then feel free to ask, as Buddhists usually do not expect that everybody knows their principles and traditions. It is common to remove shoes when entering the home or the shrine room or area set aside for meditation within the home or the room. Avoid touching any statues or images of the Buddha. Also avoid smoking in shrine rooms or areas where Buddhist statues, painting or other symbols are present. As mentioned above, in Asian homes avoid pointing with the soles of your shoes/feet towards a person or a shrine.

Death:

Apply principles of respect and dignity. Death and accepting death is a key to Buddhist belief. Many Buddhists will want to use the last moments of their lives in meditation and one should try to make this possible. According to Buddhist teachings an inner subtle consciousness may stay within the body for a while even after medicine declares a person dead. It is thus advisable to wait *at least 30 minutes* after the apparent death before touching the body of the deceased.

Buddhist funerals vary according to country of origin of the deceased. Often, Buddhists are cremated within 3-7 days after death. Usually friends and family will know about the particularities.

Always apply the principles of respect and protection. For some Buddhists it may be very important for members of the family to be present at or near the moment of death and for them to have control over the handling of the body after death.

Event planning:

Try to ensure that vegetarian and Vegan food is provided and clearly labelled. If Chinese Buddhists are present, try to ensure there is some hot food and drink available.
For long events: provision of a meditation room with facilities for kneeling and sitting (cushions, kneelers or chairs). Consult with individual Buddhists with respect to possibilities (and fire alarm risks) of burning incense.

GENERAL FAITH HEALTH WARNING:

- A little knowledge can be very dangerous!

- Treat all people of a faith as individuals and beware of generalisations.

- Be aware that there is a great diversity of belief and practise within each faith.

- Ask 'What do you do?' NOT 'Why do you do it?' Don't expect people to know and have to explain/justify WHY they do something.

- Always treat objects held to be sacred with great respect: e.g. holy books, sacred pictures, special items of clothing and jewellery, prayer beads, food and incense that may have a sacred value for the person.

Liverpool's Buddhist Community and Heritage

There are estimated to be between 500 and 1,000 practising Buddhists in Liverpool. The first Buddhist group was established about 30 years ago. Meanwhile there are groups of at least eight different traditions meeting in and around the city.

The *Chiron Centre* in Liverpool 8 provides weekly meditation classes for men in a Tibetan Buddhist tradition. The *Diamond Way Buddhist Centre* at Newsham Park follows the Karma Kagyu Tradition of Tibetan Buddhism. The *Duldzin* Centre in Sefton Park belongs to a recently established tradition called "New Kadampa Tradition". The *Theravada Buddhist* Group as well as the *Zen Buddhist Group* meet in different venues on Hope Street, while the *Serene Reflection Meditation Group* currently meet on the Wirral. Furthermore the *Dechen Community*, the *Friends of the Western Buddhist Order* and *Soka Gakkai* are present in and around Liverpool. More information on Buddhist groups in this area can be found at: www.mersey-buddhists.org

Thanks and Acknowledgements to:

Peter Malinowski	*Diamond Way Buddhist Centre*
Debbie Monks	*Duldzin Buddhist Centre*
Martin Huiskens	*Chiron Centre*
	(and Liverpool Community Spirit)

THE CHRISTIAN COMMUNITIES

Faith: **Christianity**
Faith Community: **Christians**

Holy Books/Scriptures:

The Christian scriptures, known collectively as 'The Bible' are not just one book, but a collection of writings spanning nearly a thousand years. The Bible comprises both the 'New' and the 'Old' Testaments. The Old Testament comprises a collection of the Jewish Holy Scriptures (God's revelations before Christ). The New Testament contains the distinctively Christian scriptures, including:

i The four Gospels: the four accounts of the life, teaching, death and resurrection of Jesus the Christ.

ii The Acts of the Apostles: the account of the establishment of the first Christian church communities after the resurrection of Jesus.

iii The Epistles: a series of letters written by Jesus' Apostles to provide spiritual guidance for the Christian communities.

iv The Book of Revelation: a powerful spiritual vision and guide concerning the future and the final fulfilment of humanity and the Church.

Sacred Languages:

The New Testament Scriptures were originally written in Greek and later translated into Latin. Greek remains the liturgical language of many Orthodox Churches in the East and, until fairly recently, Latin was the liturgical language of the Roman Catholic Church.

Core Belief:

Christians believe in **One God**, the Creator, the Sustainer and Lord of all that is (seen and unseen). The purpose of human life is to glorify God and participate in his redemption of creation (including humanity) from the imperfections resulting from sin.

Christianity teaches that human beings and the world have **fallen** from a state of perfection into a state of **Sin** (= falling short or 'missing the mark' of the perfect state God intends for us) caused by our wilful disobedience (rooted in pride) which separates us from God. The cost/penalty of sin is death.

Christians believe that **Redemption** from this separation/sin (and the consequent slavery to death) cannot be achieved solely through what they regard as the 'Old' Way of an outward obedience to religious practices, based on human endeavour. This Old Way can fuel rather than destroy the pride (leading to self-righteousness) that causes humanity to Fall into the state of sin.

Christianity teaches that Redemption/salvation is only achievable through **God's Grace**, which alone enables the self-emptying and self-sacrifice necessary to overcome sin/pride.

Christians believe that by becoming **Incarnate** in the life and loving self-sacrifice of **Jesus** the **Christ** (= God's Blessed/anointed one), God redeems all of humanity, pays the penalty of sin (i.e. overcomes the power of death) and opens the **New Way** (of self-sacrificial Love) for all peoples to participate in His redemptive work. Thereby God restores the possibility of becoming His **sons** and **daughters** and attaining eternal life. This is the **Good News** contained in the Gospels ('gospel' means 'good news'). The New Way is based on the new revelation (in the life, teaching and death of Jesus the Christ) of God as **Father** of all humanity whose true nature is self-giving, unconditional **love**. Christians believe that humans should be Christ-like by adopting His New Way of universal love and forgiveness.

The New Revelation of God as **Love**, is expressed through the Christian belief in the **Trinity**: God is One, but His inner nature of Love is revealed most perfectly in the loving relationship expressed between His revelations as **Father**, **Son** (Jesus Christ) and **Holy Spirit**. The Holy Spirit is the creative, loving presence of God that inspires and guides the Church (the living body of Christ) after the ascension of Christ.

Denominations:

Throughout its history, the Christian Church has developed different styles of worship and different structures of authority. The first major split was between the Western European Roman Catholic Church and the Eastern Orthodox Churches (e.g. Greek, Russian, Romanian, etc). This was largely a difference of opinion about the authority of the Bishop of Rome (the Pope).

A second major split occurred in Western Europe in the 16th century, with the formation of the Protestant Churches (who 'protested' against perceived corruptions and excess power of the Papal institution in Rome).

Many different denominations of Protestant Church, each with a distinctive mode of worship and structure of authority have evolved over recent centuries.

Annual events relating to Faith: (recognised by most denominations):

Event:	Date:	Significance:
Christmas	25th December	Festival celebrating the birth of Jesus Christ
Epiphany	6th January	Festival celebrating the manifestation of the meaning and significance of Christ (and the redemption/salvation he brings) to the Wise Men and hence to all the Gentile (non-Jewish) world.
Lent	Spring	Observing Jesus' sojourn in the wilderness- 6 weeks of prayer and fasting (beginning with Ash Wednesday) in preparation for:
Easter	Spring	The major Christian Festival, celebrating the death and resurrection of Jesus Christ (see below).
Holy Week		The last week of Lent, leading up to and including: Easter: beginning with Palm Sunday and including Maundy Thursday (when Jesus celebrated the first Eucharist, the Last Supper with his 12 disciples); Good Friday, the day he was crucified; and Easter Sunday when Christians believe he rose from the dead.
Ascension Day	Thursday, 40 days after Easter	Celebration of the day on which Jesus Christ ascended into Heaven.
Pentecost/ Whitsun	50 days after Easter	Commemorating the coming of the Holy Spirit to Christ's disciples - the Church

The growing number of evangelical churches have developed new non-liturgical festivals, such as Spring Harvest, New Wine and Soul Survivor. These are very free, open celebrations attracting large numbers of young people and promote Christian fellowship and teaching.

Daily acts of Faith/Devotion:

Prayer: Daily prayers at morning and evening and quiet reflection. Many Christians follow individual programmes of daily acts of devotion including prayer, meditation and studying Scriptures.

Sacraments: Sacraments are holy/sacred actions through which God's saving Grace is communicated. Most Christians believe in:

1. The **Holy Communion/Mass** - the re-enactment and/or remembrance of (in the powerful sense of 'making present') Christ's sharing of bread and wine, which was a symbol of his loving self-sacrifice on the cross. And also,
2. **Baptism**: originally (and still for many Christians today) the total immersion in water in the name of the Father, Son and the Holy Spirit, which symbolises death and then re-birth into the new life of the Church - the sacred body/community of believers - and the washing away of sin. Many churches later replaced total immersion with pouring of water over the head.

Roman and Anglican Catholics and Orthodox Churches believe in 7 sacraments: Holy Communion/Mass; Baptism, Confirmation, Marriage, Ordination, Confession, Penance, Extreme Unction (anointing of sick with blessed oil).

Sunday: is 'The Lord's Day', the holy day or Sabbath for most Christians when they will gather as a Church community to pray and worship God. Sunday is normally a day of rest from work. A small minority of Christians, notably Seventh Day Adventists, still maintain the Sabbath on a Saturday.

Food:

Generally, there are no universal requirements pertaining to food. Christians are not religiously forbidden from eating particular foods, other than foods used in sacrifices to other gods. Some Christian sects encourage vegetarianism and ban the use of stimulating substances and intoxicants, for example alcohol, tobacco, tea and coffee.

The period of Lent (40 days) is traditionally a time for abstinence and spiritual discipline when many Christians would fast. Moreover, fasting can be performed voluntarily at any other time of the year in preparation for the eucharist/mass, and also as an act of repentance, or an individual act of devotion. Although many Christians do not fast for Lent, followers may give-up a favoured item.

Friday was a traditional day of fasting for Christians in Britain (in commemoration of 'Good Friday': the day of Christ's Crucifixion) and this often took the form of refraining from eating meat (once a luxury for most people) other than fish (this tradition lingers on in the form of having fish on Fridays)

Greetings:
These would coincide with whatever is customary for the country. Traditional greetings include, *Peace be with you* and the old-English *Godspeed* ('May God help you on your journey through life') and *God be with you* (this is the origin of 'Goodbye').

Dress:
Apply principles of modesty and respect. There are no overall religious guidelines regarding dress, apart from the encouragement to dress modestly. However, religious leaders, priests, monks, nuns may wear distinctive, traditional garments and colours.

Speech:
Using or swearing in the name of God/Jesus Christ is blasphemous (disrespectful).
Common phrases include:
God Willing - uttered when referring to future events.
God Bless - uttered as a farewell.

Religious Symbols/Imagery:
The Cross. Images of Jesus and stories from the Bible and images of saints (often worn on pendants or rings: e.g. St George and St Christopher). Icons are a special type of painted image used in Orthodox Churches. They are hand made by monks according to strict spiritual guidelines and are venerated in both the home and in Churches as a focus for prayer and meditation. They are regarded as 'windows into heaven'.

Visiting Place of Worship:
Apply principles of modesty and respect. Christians describe the Church as the '**body of Christ**' because it is seen as the continued presence of Christ and his redemptive work in the world. The Church therefore refers to the community of believers and not the building where they happen to gather. In common usage and over time the word 'Church' has come to refer to the building where the true Church meets and worships, though many non Conformists and also some Irish Catholics prefer the term 'chapel' to denote the building. Although each building may vary in presentation from the simple to the ornate, it is usual to find a focal point: the **altar** (representing both the table of the last supper and the altar of self-sacrificing love), or the **pulpit** and find seats or rows of benches (pews) for the congregation.

During service, offerings of money may be collected: visitors can donate, but are not always expected to. There is no specific dress etiquette, though the principles of modesty and respect still apply.

It is also traditional for men to bare their heads in most places of worship and sometimes for women to cover her head. A respectful silence should be maintained.

Many Christians will bow, kneel and/or genuflect when passing in front of a crucifix on an altar and especially (in catholic and Orthodox traditions) where there is a tabernacle (an ornate box) containing the reserved sacrament (the consecrated bread 'hosts' for use in mass and which manifest or represent the very presence of Christ), which is regarded (and venerated) with utmost respect.

On entering church, many Christians dip fingers in holy water and cross themselves (reminder/renewal of Baptismal vows).

Death and Funeral Rites:
Apply principles of respect and dignity. Christianity teaches that death is not to be feared since Christ has overcome the power of death. It is traditional in Britain for Christians to dress in sombre colours for funerals. For many centuries, Christians did not allow cremation (because of the belief in bodily resurrection), but nowadays, cremation is widely accepted and practised by many Christian denominations. Bodies of the deceased should be treated with great respect.

The dying and their families may require the presence of a Priest (of their preferred denomination - but never make assumptions on this, always ask!).

Church Structures:
Orthodox, Roman Catholic, Anglican, Lutheran and many other churches follow the three-fold structure of authority:

1. Bishops: ordained priests who have oversight and guide the many individual churches (and priests/presbyters) in their given area.
2. Priests/Presbyters: the ministers for an individual church (or a number of churches). Normally ordained priests perform the Mass/Holy Communion.
3. Deacons: assist the priests/presbyters in carrying out their ministry.

In the Roman Catholic Church, priests must be celibate. In the Orthodox, Anglican and other churches a priest can marry.

In the Roman Catholic and Orthodox Churches (and some Anglican Catholic churches) only men can become priests. The Anglican and most other Protestant Churches permit women to become priests.

Many Protestant churches reject what they regard as a hierarchical structure of priesthood and are corporately governed by elected bodies, others by Pastors or leaders who develop a team approach based on owned vision and goals.

In addition to main congregational meetings and celebrations, smaller groups meetings in homes during the week have now become widely practised (similar to the early church gatherings). Sometimes these groups are called cells.

Monks and Nuns:
Throughout its history, the Christian community has had a strong and vibrant tradition of monasticism. Monks and nuns are men and women who commit themselves to intense spiritual devotion and the discipline of the three-fold vow of poverty, chastity and obedience. Many and various monastic communities have evolved, each with their own distinctive rules.

Medical Matters:
Only Jehovah's Witnesses forbid blood transfusions (a belief based upon the command 'abstain from blood', Acts 15:20). Christian Scientists have a tradition of treating disease as a spiritual phenomena and may refuse many conventional medical treatments.

Event Planning:
Avoid Sunday mornings and major festivals. However, remember that 7th day Adventist keep the Sabbath on a Saturday.
For long term events provide room for prayer.

GENERAL FAITH HEALTH WARNING:

- A little knowledge can be very dangerous!
- Treat all people of a faith as **individuals** and beware of generalisations.
- Be aware that there is a great diversity of belief and practise within each faith.
- Ask 'What do you do?' NOT 'Why do you do it?' Don't expect people to know and have to explain/justify WHY they do something.
- Always treat objects held to be sacred with great respect: e.g. holy books, sacred pictures, special items of clothing and jewellery, prayer beads, food, incense and water that may have a sacred value for the person.

Liverpool's Christian Communities and Heritage

Ancient: Roman Catholic (Pre-Reformation):
St Patrick: this Celtic Saint preached from a point called St Patrick's Hill in present day Marybone, Liverpool in AD 432. A cross marked the spot and the Church of Holy Cross (now demolished) in Marybone commemorated the site.

The Parish church of St Mary in Walton goes back to Saxon times (recorded in Doomsday Book of 1086). There are records going back to 1150 of Benedictine monks residing at Birkenhead Priory. The Abbot had a house in Water St. Liverpool. They ferried people across the Mersey.

In the 13th Century the small stone chapel of St Mary del Key stood at the current site of Our Lady and St Nicholas Church, which is now the Parish Church of Liverpool. The chapel contained an image of the Virgin Mary and sailors prayed for safe sea journeys. In 1361 the Black Death resulted in the need for more burial sites. St Nicholas Church was established close to St Mary del Key. Eventually St Nicholas thrived and it became a well established church. Post Reformation, it became Church of England. It was subject to St. Mary's Walton until 1699. Only in 1913 was it designated as the official Parish Church of Liverpool. In the 1940's a bomb destroyed the Church and it was re-built.

Reformation (1532):
Has its roots in the 14th century attempts to reform the Roman Catholic Church in the light of certain perceived corruptions of its privileged position of power/wealth in society (e.g. John Wycliffe martyred for trying to translate Holy Scripture into English to make it more accessible to the common people).

It was Martin Luther and John Calvin who led the Reformation in Europe (the Lutheran Church is a large Protestant Church in many Western European countries: there is a German Lutheran Church in L8). The reform of the Christian Church in England and Wales came with Henry VIII's break from Rome and his declaration that he was the Head of the Church in England, not the Pope. However, the Church of England remained Catholic in its theology and worship. Pressure from the Protestant reformers during the time of King Edward VI, Queen Elizabeth and later, led to the partial reform of worship and the establishment of the Book of Common Prayer, which still remains an official guide for worship in the Anglican communion (= all the world-wide Churches that developed from the Church of England).

Roman Catholics, in spite of persecution, continued to practice and often had to meet in secret (Speke Hall contains secret hiding holes for Catholic Priests dating from the times of the persecution of Catholics).

Other, more radical Protestant reformers established independent churches with greater emphasis upon the authority of Holy Scripture and rejection of church hierarchies, priesthood, bishops and the more ritualistic, sacramental forms of worship.

They were persecuted and discriminated against. In Liverpool they settled outside the city for protection and security: e.g. The Ancient Chapel of Toxteth (which is now a branch of the Unitarian church) was a dissenters chapel built in 1618 by members of the **Toxteth Park Puritan Colony**, a settlement of puritans from Bolton on the disembarked royal deer park. 25 farms were laid out on land that had the advantage of not coming under Church of England jurisdiction. Their presence is also remembered in names in the area -Jericho farm, River Jordan & Holyland.

The largest **Free-Churches** (= the Protestant Churches that are free and independent of the Church of England) in Liverpool today are the Methodists, the Baptists and the United Reformed Church (formed from a union of Presbyterians and Congregationalists). The Methodist Church resulted from a split from the Church of England. The beautiful old Methodist Central Hall on Renshaw Street (recently converted into a pub/club Barcelona) gives an indication of the great size and importance of this community in the past. Baptist Churches, both living and redundant can be found all over the City.

For centuries, the Quaker (Society of Friends) Christian community, though small, has had a major influence in social reform; pioneering in the long struggles to establish democracy, women's rights and abolish slavery.

Liverpool also has historic Welsh and Scottish Presbyterian communities (the magnificent ruins of the 'Welsh Cathedral' on Princes Road and also St Andrews Church on Rodney St reflect their former glory).

Liverpool also has a very distinctive history of Brethren Assemblies (run by elders) who experienced remarkable growth during the 20th century.

The fastest growing Christian communities today are the independent **House Churches** and **Charismatic** and **Evangelical Churches**, for example the Frontline Church, Wavertree and Bridge Chapel, Garston. Many of these in Liverpool now have links with 'Together for the Harvest', which is a network of church leaders, which is officially linked to the national Evangelical Alliance.

The Reformation also began a long history of conflict and tensions between Catholics and Protestants. Once the Church of England was fully established, Catholic churches and open Catholic worship were banned. The ancient Parish churches of England and Wales became Church of England.

The Church of England:

is the Established Church (established by law and tradition as the 'official' religion of the nation). The whole country and therefore the City of Liverpool, is divided up into Church of England Parishes. As the Established Church, the Church of England has certain state privileges and duties and is still partly controlled by the state (the Crown appoints Archbishops, Bishops and Deans). Everyone living in the parish, no matter what their faith background, is entitled to draw upon the services of their Parish church if they wish. The Church of England is part of the world-wide Anglican communion.

Roman Catholic (Post Reformation):

Liverpool's largest faith community is the Roman Catholic community. More commonly called 'Catholic', many people still use the term 'Roman Catholic' to distinguish it from the broader 'catholic' church, which refers to all Christian churches. The term catholic is Latin in origin and means *universal.*

Roman Catholics were not allowed to establish new Churches until the Catholic Emancipation, which began in the 18th century but was not completed until the 19th century. The first Roman Catholic church in Liverpool built since the Reformation was St Mary's, built in Edmund Street, Marybone, in the early eighteenth century (1707). The oldest standing Catholic Church today is St Peter's Seel St. (closed in 1978).

Liverpool has a long history of Irish immigration. Large numbers of Irish (and Italian) Catholic immigrants settled in Marybone and also the Vauxhall and Everton districts. Saint Anthony's church, Scotland Road, has a particularly rich heritage going back to Fr. Jean Baptiste Antoine Gerardot who founded the parish in 1804. Fr Gerardot was a French èmigrè priest who fled from the French revolution. In the 1840s, the priests of the parish ministered to the thousands of Irish immigrants who fled their native Ireland to escape the potato famine - sadly many of them died as a result of the typhus epidemic - in 1847 alone, over 2,300 were buried in St Anthony's. To mark the occasion of its 200th anniversary and to honour the memory of those parishioners and the Irish immigrants interred in the Crypt, Fr Tom Williams (now Bishop Williams) built the visitor Centre at St Anthony's, which also houses a computer data base of parish records for those who wish to trace their ancestors.

The conflict between Catholic and Protestant communities often became focused around and exacerbated by the conflict between England and Ireland; hence the clashes between Protestant and Catholic communities in Liverpool around the Orange Day parades (the Protestant community's celebrations of the Battle of the Boyne in which King William defeated the Catholic Jacobite forces in the 17th century).

The Greek Orthodox Church: large numbers of Greeks and Greek Cypriots settled in Liverpool in the 19th and 20th centuries. St Nicholas Orthodox Church on Princes Road/Berkeley Street **(consecrated 1871)** is the centre of Liverpool's Orthodox community. Orthodox Christians place great emphasis upon sacramental worship and give high status and importance to Priests and Bishops (other Orthodox Churches include the Russian, Bulgarian, Romanian and Armenian; also, similar in structure, theology and worship are the ancient Coptic Churches of Egypt and Ethiopia and the Assyrian church of Iraq).

The (Gustav Adolphekirke) Scandinavian Church (consecrated 1873): situated on Park Road, this church serves the needs of the Scandinavian community and seafarers.

Mormons: The Church of Jesus Christ of Latter Day Saints: founded by Joseph Smith in New York in 1830. Mormons believe he received a revelation (the Book of Mormon) from God to guide the Christian community.

Following persecutions, his successor, Brigham Young, led the Mormon community to establish their holy land in Utah with its centre in Salt Lake City. They have 4 Holy Books: the Bible, the Book of Mormon, Doctrine and Covenants and The Pearl of Great Price which was first published in Liverpool in 1851.

Liverpool was the location for the first missionaries to come to Europe and also the first emigration of Mormon converts to the USA. The Liverpool Mormon community first met in the Music Hall on Bold Street, where Brigham Young preached. Many traditional Christians see Mormon beliefs as so different from their creed, that they don't regard them as Christians. Mormons deny this. There are approx, 800 Mormons in Liverpool today.

Jehovah's Witnesses (JWs) an apocalyptical group established in 1897 by Charles Taze Russell in the USA. They reject the Christian doctrine of the Trinity and preach the imminence of armageddon and the establishment of God's kingdom on earth (and the salvation of the 144,000 elect). They pledge loyalty to a New World Theocracy and neutrality in secular political process. JWs practise baptism, but reject most other rites and the priesthood, placing authority in a system of 'Elders'.

In Liverpool it is estimated (according to the 2001 census) that over 79% of the population consider themselves as Christian.

Thanks and acknowledgements to:

Mr. Ultan Russell	Church and Society, Liverpool Diocese
Rev. Martyn Newman	Churches Together in the Merseyside Region
Canon Michael Wolfe	Merseyside Inter-faith Group
Mgr. John Devine	Churches Officer for the North West
Howard Garner	Frontline Church, Wavertree

THE HINDU COMMUNITY

Faith: **Hinduism:** name given in the nineteenth century to the coalition of religion, which existed in India.

Faith Community: **Hindu** (A Persian word which is from the Sanskrit 'Sindu'/ 'river', refering to those people belonging to the Indus valley). The tradition refers to itself as 'Sanatana Dharma', 'The Eternal Path for Righteousness'.

Holy Books/Scriptures:

The Vedas: ('Veda' = 'to know'), which for Hindus contain eternal truths. They are made up of four collections of texts. The Samhitas, Brahmanas, Aranyakas and Upanishads. They are called 'shruti' or heard, indicating their divine origin and status. There are the great epics: the Mahabharata and the Ramayana. The Puranas and Agamas contain many short aphorisms called sutras and are collectively known as smriti.

Sacred Languages:

Sanskrit. The language is deemed Holy in itself.

Core Belief:

Hinduism is a journey into soul/self and the discovery there of a most fundamental truth that at the heart of our self (= the *Atman*) there is God (= *Brahman*). Hinduism provides many ways or paths for the individual and community to practically realise this truth and achieve liberation (= *Moksha*) from the ignorance, suffering and limitations of our world and the cycles of re-birth called *samsara* (lit. 'bondage').

Understanding and following **Dharma** (= our duty in life according to our age, sex, and social class) is the key to success.

Hindus believe that God is One who manifests in many different forms in different eras to uphold Dharma. Devotion to those forms is also a key element of religious life.

Re-birth of the individual soul is determined by the law of **karma** (the law of cause and effect with respect to our actions/thoughts and their consequences) including the degree of success in following Dharma.

Annual events relating to Faith:

Event:	Date:	Significance:
Ugadi/Gud Parva	March-April	For many, this marks the beginning of the Hindu New Year.
Holi (Spring)	Spring	Last full moon day celebrates the welcoming of spring: A joyous Festival where all grievances are forgotten and all people regardless of race, gender or class sprinkle each other with coloured powder or liquid.
Shivarati/Mahashivarati	Feb/March	Worship dedicated to Lord Shiva. Worshippers spend nights at Temple singing and chanting. Milk is poured continuously as an offering onto the linga, the symbolic form of lord Shiva. Among some families there is also a tradition of fasting.
Rama Navami	March-April	Celebrates the birth (7th Incarnation) of Lord Rama as an avatar. Hindus fast on this occasion and the Ramayana, the epic of Rama and Sita is read aloud in Temples.
Jan Mashtami	August-September	Celebrates the birth of Krishna (8thIncarnation) of the deity Vishnu. Worshippers fast until midnight, when a symbolic image of Krishna is welcomed into Temple with flowers and rejoicing.
Navaratri	October	Celebration of the victory of good over evil and the Return of Sri Ramachandra to Ayodhya after conquering the evil demon Ravana.
Divali/Deepwali ('Festival of Lights')	Oct-early Nov	To honour the deity Goddess Lakshmi. Celebrates the symbolic reunion of Rama and his wife Sita. Family festival celebrating the victory of light over darkness and knowledge over ignorance. For some Hindus the festival marks the beginning of the New Year.

Daily acts of Faith:
Generally, daily acts are of personal devotion alone, or with others. Practice of domestic worship is widespread. Most Hindus have a shrine or small area for worship containing pictures and idols (sacred images or figures that represent deities). In addition to private worship large gathering for worship may also take place in private homes. Devotion in Temple and at home include; meditation (*japa*), singing songs (*bhajans*) and chanting mantras (holy words/phrases), worship of and prayer to (*puja*) the idol of the deity (*murti*), study of sacred texts and sacred ceremonies.

Food:
Many Hindus are vegetarian or Vegan, (no meat, fish, eggs or anything produced from animals). Many prefer to refrain from alcohol and onions and garlic. Food is eaten with right hand only. Hindus do not eat beef (sacred animal) or pork.

Greetings:
To greet a person, friend or pay respect to an elder or deity: join the hands with palms together, bow in front of them and say *namaska, pranam namaste* (or *namaste* for short) which means reverence and salutation to the person. Namaste = 'I bow to/respect/acknowledge the God (the Divine soul) in you'.

Dress:
Principles of modesty and respect apply. The only religious guidelines regarding dress are that Hindus are not permitted to wear leather. In the Temple some cover their heads and all would remove footwear and dress smartly when attending Temple. There are regional variations on headwear e.g. in parts of South India, a woman covers her head as sign of being a widow).

The *Bindi* or *tilaka* has become very fashionable, but it has a deep religious significance (representing the third eye of spiritual perception and/or and female power of God).
In Britain, Hindus often wear Western style clothing, but may also wear a dhoti (knee length piece of cloth tied around the waist) or loose cotton trousers. Men may also wear kurta (silk or cotton knee length loose long shirt) or *chunidar* (longer dress garment).

Jewellery is popular and carers should always seek permission before having to remove any items of jewellery that may have a sacred value/symbolism.

Speech:
Consideration must be shown with regard the use of offensive language or behaviour. No swearing or name calling (e.g. 'swine' and 'dog' are particularly offensive).

Elders are generally called 'Aunty' or 'Uncle', rather than by their personal name, as sign of respect. It is traditional to add the suffix 'ji' to the name of elders, teachers, etc as a mark of respect.

Religious Symbols/Imagery:
The images of Gods in Temple and home are believed to be alive and must be shown respect.

Images of deities in Temple and home are sacred and should be respected at all times and not be touched.

OM: Most common and powerful Hindu symbol is that of OM (sometimes spelt AUM in English). It is the sacred symbol of Brahman, the supreme Godhead and is used in mediation and mantras.

Swastika: a very ancient Indian symbol (taken and reversed by the Nazis) symbolising the auspicious power and blessings of God.

Shree: a symbol of Lakshmi, the goddess of wealth of knowledge.

Visiting Place of Worship:
Apply general principles of cleanliness, modesty and respect: Footwear should be removed before entering the Temple (respect and avoiding bringing dirt from outside into the holy environment). Ideally, one should wash before entering the Temple. Hindu temples are richly decorated with pictures and with 'idols' of the many deities of Hindu tradition. All should be respected and treated as if they were real: Hindus believe that the images communicate and bring the real presence of the deity before the worshipper (they are specially consecrated according to ancient Vedic rituals). Worshippers bow before the images and may touch the steps in the temple as a sign of respect.

Food and money offerings are placed before the deities. Food and flower offerings should not be touched.

It is polite and respectful to accept the prashad (food offered and blessed by the deities) when it is offered. Smart and modest dress should be worn.

Visiting the Home:
Apply general principles of cleanliness, modesty and respect. Footwear is removed before entering the home.

Avoid physical contact with members of the opposite sex. Eat with right hand. It would be impolite to refuse food and drink offered. Food should not be touched with the left hand. Respect for elders is paramount.

Gender Issues:

Hindus believe both sexes should be treated equally and neither is superior. Hindus recognize that God is equally manifested in female as well as male forms.

Men and women sit separately in Temple. There is a female priest in Liverpool.

Physical contact between male and female should be avoided. In a caring or hospital situation, it is usually preferable to have carers of the same sex, especially when physical contact cannot be avoided.

Death:

Principles of respect and dignity apply. Dying may wish to be comforted by hearing holy scriptures read. Families generally wish to handle and lay out their dead. Death seen as liberation and bodies are generally cremated. After being ritually bathed, the body is placed on open wooden pyre (in India) facing north or south. After spiritual chants and worship, the eldest son (or other relative) lights some kindling and walks around pyre chanting prayers for the deceased soul before lighting the pyre. Holy water from the river Ganges is sprinkled. It is traditional to take food to the family of the bereaved.

Priests and Pundits:

Pundit: a learned person who has studied the Hindu scriptures at a *GuruKala* (Sanskrit university in India). A qualified Pundit is always a Priest as well.

Priest: a person who is qualified in performing the sacred rituals associated with the 16 stages of life (called *Samskaras*, including conception, birth, naming, first day out, the Sacred thread initiation ceremony, marriage and death). Priests are often called into houses to perform rituals and they conduct the ceremonies in the temple. Priests are not necessarily Pundits.

According to tradition, both Priests and Pundits are drawn from the *Brahmin* (the highest, priestly) caste, but there are exceptions and controversy concerning the application of this tradition.

Event Planning:

Avoid clashes with major festivals.
Ensure good washing facilities are available.
Clearly label all food.
Showers may be regarded as more preferable than baths (washing with running water that carries away dirt is considered cleaner and more effective than a bath).

GENERAL FAITH HEALTH WARNING:

- A little knowledge can be very dangerous!
- Treat all people of a faith as **individuals** and beware of generalisations.
- Be aware that there is a great diversity of belief and practise within each faith.
- Ask 'What do you do?' NOT 'Why do you do it?' Don't expect people to know and have to explain/justify WHY they do something.
- Always treat objects held to be sacred with great respect: e.g. holy books, sacred pictures, special items of clothing and jewellery, prayer beads, food and incense that may have a sacred value for the person.

Liverpool's Hindu Community and Heritage:

The Hindu community in Liverpool goes back many decades. Hindus were amongst some of the Asian visors and settlers in Liverpool between the world wars. However, there may have been Hindus who accompanied Liverpool's earliest Asian residents, the Parsees who came in the 1850's (see Appendix on page 48).

Liverpool was also blessed by a visit of Ram Mohan Roy, the great Hindu Indian reformer, sage and writer in 1833. A Hindu Temple and cultural centre was opened in 1958 on Botanic Road. Vijaya Lakshmi Pandit, the wife of Prime Minister Nehru of India, visited the Centre in the same year. In 1976, the building was sold to the Sikh community and a new and present Hindu Cultural Centre and Mandir was opened in Edge Lane. As well as all the religious ceremonies, the Centre holds many social, educational and cultural events for people of all ages from the community, including Youth Clubs, Senior Citizens clubs and Women's groups.

It is estimated that Liverpool's Hindu community numbers around 1,000 people.

Thanks and acknowledgements to:

Dr Ajit Kumar: Centre for Vedic Studies
Bisakha Sarkar: Indian Arts Practioner
(and Liverpool Community Spirit)

THE JEWISH COMMUNITY

Faith: **Judaism**
Faith Community: **Jews/Jewish**

Holy Books/Scriptures:

Judaism is rooted in the **Torah**, which contains 613 commandments, or *Mitzvot*, which are seen as the revelation of G-d and the basis of the covenantal relationship between G-d and the people.

The Torah consists of the five books of Moses:

- Genesis
- Exodus
- Leviticus
- Numbers
- Deuteronomy

The Jewish scriptures begin with Joshua, Judges, Samuel and Kings and other texts like Ruth and Esther, and include books known as the Nevi'im, the Prophets such as Isaiah, Jeremiah, Ezekiel and others. The last section is called '*Ketuvim*' ('writings') such as the Psalms, Proverbs and Songs of Solomon.

Talmud

This contains the *Mishna*, which is the basis of the discussion on all matters of the 'Oral Law', and only put into writing because of the weakness of generations who would have ultimately forgotten it. The *Gemara* is a detailed commentary on the Mishna, and a record of all discussions that took place in the academies of Jewish learning.

Midrash

Midrash is the rabbinic teaching which comprises parables, legends and stories from early 'rabbis' (teachers), as well as extremely difficult passages open to interpretation. It is a part of the tradition that has been handed down since the Torah was given.

Sacred Languages:

Hebrew is the language of the Jewish Scripture and the main language of worship, written from right to left.

Core Belief:

Belief in **One** G-d, who is Creator and Lord of the universe, whose Will is supreme and is revealed in His laws to guide humanity to their true calling and fulfilment. The essence of G-d's guiding Laws is revealed to humanity through the Torah given through His chosen prophet Moses. The Jewish people are called by G-d to provide an exemplary life of **holiness** by following and fulfilling all G-d's commands. In the Torah Jews learn to love G-d through study, prayer and celebrating holy days. Emphasis is upon living a righteous life and fulfilling one's duty in this world. The Torah, with its **613** laws is seen as the tree of life - the source of all human blessings and fulfilment.

The Jewish people are considered to be called by G-d to be a holy people, separated and called by G-d through **Covenants** with prophets Abraham, Isaac, Israel and Moses. This expression 'Chosen People' means chosen for responsibility. This calling is a great blessing, despite the extremely difficult episodes in our history for which we believe G-d has His reasons, however difficult to bear. Jews view their **Holy Land** - Israel as an integral part of their calling and duty to be a holy people and to look forward to the time when, according to all accounts, the Messiah of the Davidic dynasty will arrive and the third Temple will be re-built in Jerusalem, bringing with it times of **peace** for all mankind.

Annual events relating to Faith: Judaism follows a 13 month lunar calendar.

Event:	Date:	Significance:
Days of Awe		
Rosh Hashanah	Two days in Autumn	Celebrating the New Year. Time of reflection and penitence.
Yom Kippur/ Day of Atonement	Autumn	A major annual event, where a twenty-five hour fast is observed in conjunction with Torah Law. This day is a serious day when believers atone for all their sins
Three foot festivals		
Pesach/Passover	lasts 8 days of Spring	Festival celebrating the ancestral escape/Exodus from Egypt after enslavement and oppression by the Pharaoh. During this period no leavened bread is eaten as a reminder of the Exodus where those fleeing were unable to prepare bread with yeast.
Shavuot	Summer	Commemorating the receiving of the Torah at Sinai.
Sukkot	Autumn	Commemorating the wanderings of the People of Israel in the desert where they enjoyed G-d's protection.
Minor Festivals include:		
Chanukah	Nov/Dec	A festival of Light, remembering the re-dedication/purification of the Jerusalem temple after it had been desecrated by the Ancient Greeks.
Purim	Spring	A reminder of the story of Esther, who saved the Jewish people from genocide at the hands of a corrupt Persian official.
Tishah B'Av	Late summer	Commemorating the historical destruction of the Great Jerusalem Temples in 586 BCE and 72AD.

Daily acts of Faith:
Shema
The most common daily prayer is called the Shema (lit: 'Hear'), which is a fundamental affirmation of faith:
'Hear O Israel, the Lord our G-d is One G-d. You shall love the Lord your G-d with all your heart, soul and strength.'

Practising Jews pray a minimum of three times a day: morning, afternoon and evening.
The heart of much daily devotion is the reciting of **Blessings**: giving thanks to G-d for everything and every event in the day, beginning with waking up and blessing G-d for restoring our soul after sleep.

Blessings begin: *Baruch atar Adonai, Elohenu Melech Halam....* = 'Blessed are You Oh Lord, King of the Universe....'

Weekly acts of Faith/Devotion:
Sabbath:
Sabbath is the great day of worship/Holy Day/Day of rest (doing no creative work) from sunset on Friday evening until night Saturday evening.

It is a day of pleasure with all the family, prayers, celebrating the goodness of life, rest and attendance at synagogue. Strictness of observance depends upon degree of orthodoxy. For the observant, shops and businesses close, money put away (even small change from pockets). People only walk if they go out. Nothing is to be carried from the house into public domain and strict distance from daily transactions of consumer society is maintained. All cooking is done in advance and food is left on a covered stove. Many homes install a Sabbath catering urn to supply hot water and lights are either left on or time-switched according to requirements. Sabbath rules must only be broken for genuine life-threatening conditions.

Food:
Jews are required to uphold '*kashrut*' - a series of dietary laws, which refer to the provision of 'kosher' food (food prepared in a special way). **Kosher** food is believed to elevate the soul to a higher spiritual level. In general, Jews do not eat pork, rabbit or shellfish and do not mix meat with dairy products at the same meal.

All meat must be slaughtered in a special manner by trained professionals (animals must be healthy; knives must be razor sharp; all blood must be removed by draining, salting and washing the meat). Kosher food is widely available. Diary products and meat must be separated at all times. All food, including certain fruit and vegetables must also be kosher and this means that its preparation must have been supervised and approved by a Jewish authority (the Beth Din). All foods must be properly washed to ensure no insect remains are present; eggs also have to be checked to ensure that there is no blood present in them; dough must have a portion separated, blessed and then given symbolically to priests (now actually thrown away because, as there is no temple, but these rules are not fully operative). Wine should also be kosher.

Greetings:
Shalom a Lechem -'Peace be with you'
A Lechem Shalom - 'Peace be with you'

Dress:
Orthodox women/girls are meant to keep body and limbs covered, and married women are meant to cover their hair. Men also cover their heads, often with a small skull cap- to show their submission to G-d. A **tallit** (prayer shawl) may be worn (reminder of G-d's law).

Speech:
Being charged with special duties, believers are meant to be heedful of their mouths, so that a mouth that emits holy prayer etc. also speaks in a clean and befitting manner.

Religious Symbols/Imagery:
Jewish symbols include: the **Menorah** (7 branched candle-stick), the Shield of David/Star of David and the Mezuzah (a parchment scroll in a small hollow box containing the first paragraph of the Shema placed on the doorframe of every room excluding bathrooms and toilets.

Visiting Place of Worship:
The Synagogue: This is the Jewish place of communal worship, prayer and study. There is inside a raised platform with a curtained alcove. Behind the curtain are doors of the Holy **Ark** containing the handwritten scrolls of the five books of Moses. The scrolls are the Synagogue's most precious possession. An ornate lamp hangs from the ceiling, which is kept alight to remind all worshippers of the light that burned perpetually in the Great Temple and is a reminder to worshippers of the constant presence of G-d. The '**mezuzah**' is hung on internal doors of the synagogue (and also on the right-hand doorposts of Jewish homes),

- Visitors are asked to avoid taking non-kosher food into the synagogue.
- Preferable for visitors to dress modestly with arms and legs covered.
- In orthodox synagogues women cover their heads, and men and boys also cover their heads when visiting all synagogues.
- In most synagogues women and men sit separately.
- Visitors are not expected to join in with worship, but are welcome to do so if they wish. After the service, (Kiddush) sanctification by blessing may be said over breads and wine and shared. Visitors are welcome to share also.

Gender issues:
Orthodox married women cover their hair. During the service in Synagogue men and women sit separately. Orthodox men and women should not touch unless of married status or related.

For more Orthodox traditions, physical contact between members of the opposite sex is prohibited.

In a caring or hospital situation, it is usually preferable to have carers of the same sex, especially when physical contact cannot be avoided.

Visiting the Home:
Principles of respect and cleanliness apply. Members of the Jewish faith will customarily touch the mezuzah on the right hand doorpost of the home (and often rooms within it) as they enter and leave. The mezuzah contains a small parchment scroll with verse from the holy Torah (including the 'shema'). They serve as a good reminder to keep G-d in one's mind and heart in one's 'going out and coming in'. Hospitality is a great spiritual virtue and it is polite to accept what is offered in its name.

Death:
Jewish tradition stipulates that funerals/burials should take place very quickly: if possible, within 24 hours of death, though not on a Sabbath.
Orthodox Jews are always buried. Liberal Jews permit cremation. Funeral ceremonies are very plain and usually avoid the donation of flowers. Traditionally there is a seven-day mourning period with prayers in the house of the mourners. Members of the community take food to the house of mourning.

Rabbis and Priests:

Since the destruction of the Temple in Jerusalem, the leadership role of priests no longer exists. The communities and worship and rituals are led by Rabbis: learned men who have studied scriptures and the Law at Rabbinical colleges. The memory and tradition of the priesthood lingers on in traditions such as the descendants of the Cohens (the Priestly 'caste' of the ancient Jewish community) and the Levites (the descendant of the tribe of Levi who assisted the Cohens) having precedence in reciting the Torah in the synagogue services.

Event Planning:

Ensure that there are no clashes with the Sabbath (sunset on Friday to nightfall on Saturday) and High Holy Days/major festivals.

Cater for Jewish food needs and make sure food is labelled clearly (remember, for Orthodox Jews ALL food must be kosher - and hence prepared under authorised supervision - and this includes basics such as bread, fruit and vegetables). Wine must be kosher.

Try to ensure clean washing facilities are available for prayer and or any food preparation/consumption.

Accommodate for prayer times.

GENERAL FAITH HEALTH WARNING:

- A little knowledge can be very dangerous!
- Treat all people of a faith as **individuals** and beware of generalisations.
- Be aware that there is a great diversity of belief and practise within each faith.
- Ask 'What do you do?' NOT 'Why do you do it?' Don't expect people to know and have to explain/justify WHY they do something.
- Always treat objects held to be sacred with great respect: e.g. holy books, sacred pictures, special items of clothing (e.g. prayer shawls and tefillin) and jewellery, prayer beads, food and drink that may have a sacred value for the person.

Liverpool's Jewish Community and Heritage

Liverpool's Jewish community claims to be the first and most influential in Northern England, founded by immigrant peddlers in the mid - 18th Century. We are blessed with a particularly rich Jewish heritage.

The first 'synagogue' was a rented house in Turtle Court near the Customs house (1775).

Next, in 1789 a rented house at 133 Upper Frederick Street.

The first purpose-built synagogue was in Seel Street, consecrated in 1808. It was the first synagogue to deliver sermons in the English language.

In the 19th century, Liverpool became a major staging post for many Jewish refugees who fled persecution and poverty in Central and Eastern Europe. Over 5,000 Jews stayed in Liverpool.

The Liverpool Jewish community became national pioneers in providing both social care and education. The Hebrew Philanthropic Society was founded in 1811 and Liverpool's Jews pioneered the development of charitable and educational institutions in the UK.

In 1841 the Liverpool Hebrew Education Institution was established, including an infant department (in 1873), a Clothing Society (1866) and a Soup Fund (1870). In 1852, it moved to a permanent school building next to the synagogue in Hope Place.

Charles Mosley was Liverpool's first Jewish mayor (1863). In 1838 a number of the community split to form a 'New Hebrew Congregation' that met first in Hanover Street and then, in 1857, built its own synagogue in Hope Place.

The world-renowned Liverpool Old Hebrew Congregation Synagogue on Princes Road was consecrated in September 1873. This is an architectural gem in the heart of our city and welcomes visitors of all faith backgrounds. At its height (in 1914) the Jewish community grew to around 11,000 people.

At the end of the 18th century and beginning of the 19th, there was a distinctive Jewish quarter in the cheaper houses around the Brownlow Hill, Paddington, Crown St and Islington districts. This ever expanding community of less economically privileged East European immigrants often formed their own societies and started up new synagogue congregations in Kirkdale, Islington, Russell Street, Shaw Street, Crown St and Walnut Street.

A Jewish Lads Brigade was formed in 1897 (the first in the provinces). A Girls club and a Jewish Working Men's club were also established.

Russian immigrants also inspired a strong Zionist movement in Liverpool. It eventually established a base at 8 Princes Road. As the Jewish community became wealthier and more established, many migrated to Sefton Park, Wavertree and Mossley Hill areas.

In 1937 the New Hebrew Congregation moved to a beautiful new synagogue on Greenbank Drive. The Brownlow Hill congregation moved to Arundel Avenue.

In 1938 the Childwall synagogue opened in Dunbabin Road.

From 1939 right up to 1960 a progressive Jewish community (begun in 1928) established a congregation that met in the Hope Place synagogue. In 1960 it moved to an old vicarage in Wavertree, adding a purpose-built synagogue in 1964.

The old Jewish community around Princes Rd and Hope Place remained vibrant until after the second world war. After the 2nd World War, the Jewish community centred around the suburbs of Childwall, Allerton and Woolton.
King David School opened in 1956 (the first Jewish Secondary school opened under the 1944 Education Act). In 1964 the Jewish Primary School at Hope Place moved to the King David site in Childwall.
Harold House was also built as the new focus of Jewish Youth and community activities. A new Allerton Hebrew Congregation synagogue was opened in Mather Avenue in 1960. Over the past 30 years, the community has considerably declined in numbers and is now estimated to be around 3,000.

The Jewish Representative Council (the umbrella organisation for all of Liverpool's Jewish congregations and community organisations) is facing an uphill struggle to try to reverse this decline in the face of Liverpool's general economic decline and mass depopulation.

Some famous Liverpool Jews:
David Lewis (founder of Lewis' Department Store - UK's first); Frankie Vaughan (singer/entertainer); Edwina Currie and Louise Ellman (politicians); Alexie Sayle (comedian); Ian Broudie (Lightning Seeds pop star who wrote England football song 'Three Lions on Our Shirt').

Thanks and acknowledgements to:

Rabbi Cofnas:	*Rabbi, Childwall Synagogue*
Avril Lewis:	*Jewish Education Resource Centre, Harold House*
Es Rosen:	*Former Director, Jewish Youth and Community Centre, Harold House*
Cecil Moss:	*Liverpool Old Hebrew Congregation Synagogue*
Bill Williams:	*Former Curator of Manchester Jewish Museum) and author of, Liverpool: A Pictorial History.*

THE MUSLIM COMMUNITY

Faith: **Islam** (lit. 'Submission/surrender to God's will').

Faith Community: **Muslim.** A Muslim is one who has submitted his/her will to Allah. All humans are created as Khalifah = agents/representatives of God on earth.

Holy Books/Scriptures/Traditions:

Holy Qur'an (*Qur'an* = 'recitation'): this is the collection of the 114 suras (chapters) revealed to the Prophet Muhammad pbuh (via the agency of the Angel Gabriel) over a period of 23 years. Muslims believe the Qur'an to be the only divine revelation that has been preserved intact. It is believed to be the final and most perfect and complete of all God's revelations. Therefore, the Qur'an is treated with the utmost respect and reverence, e.g. recited daily, often bound in elaborate covers/cloth and, in a Muslim household, always given a place of honour (e.g. placed on the top of a bookshelf higher than any other books).

Sunnah: this refers to the traditions of what the Prophet Muhammad (pbuh) said and did. They are based upon:
Hadith: these are the sayings of Prophet Muhammad (pbuh) recorded by his companions and later written down and collected.
The sunnah and hadith are the major sources for the practical interpretation and application of the Qur'an in every day life and, thereby:

Shari'ah: this is the Islamic law governing every aspect of human life to ensure that it is carried out in tune/accordance with God's Will.

Sacred Languages: Intrinsically Arabic is no more sacred than any other language (all languages and all people belong to God), but it acquired the status of a sacred language because God chose to reveal His final message to humanity in the language of His final Messenger, Muhammad (pbuh). In translation, finer shades of meaning are lost.

Core Belief:

Human beings are created to worship and glorify **Allah** (God). All humanity is born 'Muslim', i.e. with their nature directed toward God and to realising their true self and potential (*fitra*).

The opposite of a Muslim is a **Kafir** : from root *kufur* ('to cover'), i.e. one who has covered up their true nature and submitted themselves to something less than God (i.e. less than Perfect, True and Good).
It is only through complete submission/surrender of the self to the Will of Allah (God), as revealed to the Prophet Muhammad (pbuh) in the Qur'an and as manifested in the Sunnah, that true Peace, security and fulfilment can be attained in human life.

How does one become a Muslim and submit ones will to Allah?

1. Literally: recite the *Khalimah* with correct knowledge and intention in front of reliable Muslim witnesses. The Khalimah = the essential statement of Islamic faith 'There is no deity but God and Muhammad is the messenger of God'

2. Practically: in order to do this it is necessary to seek and follow knowledge and guidance from Allah, via the revelation of His Will for human beings, as communicated through His Prophets and Messengers.

Iman - Religious Faith/knowledge which, in Islam comprises six core beliefs:

1. God's Oneness/unity (**Tawhid**): To be convinced that God exists and that He is One, without partner, likeness or similarity. From His Oneness/unity follows all God's other worshipful qualities and perfections (Muslims believe God reveals 99 of His qualities to humanity: the most frequently referred to are His Compassion and His Mercy).

2. **His Angels**: Angels are created from rarefied light as God's agents/intermediaries. Many Muslims also believe in Jinn, which are mentioned in the Qur'an and are created from fire and (unlike Angels) have free-will and are more unpredictable in their nature. All this hidden realm of creation is nevertheless completely under God's direction and control. Belief in Jinn is not an article of faith.

3. **His Books**: out of His Mercy and compassion, God reveals His will to guide humanity at all times and in all places. The most important revelations are recorded in the form of books (including the scrolls given to Abraham, the Torah to Moses, the Psalms to David, the Gospel to Jesus and finally and most perfectly, the Qur'an to Muhammad pbuh).

4. **His Prophets and Messengers**: God provides inspired human beings for all times and places and peoples to guide them and to reveal His will for them. Prophets include Adam, Noah, Abraham, Ishmael, Isaac, Jacob, Moses, Elijah, John the Baptist, Jesus and, finally, Muhammad (pbuh). Those prophets who were privileged enough to have been chosen to receive one of the books of God, are called Messengers. Muhammad (pbuh) is believed to be the final and most perfect Messenger.

5. **Day of Judgment**: all humanity will be brought to account for their actions before God and judged according to His Mercy and Justice.

6. Belief in **Divine Predestination**: God is in complete control of all events (a source of great consolation in hard times).

The '**Five Pillars of Islam**' are the fundamental practices which literally uphold the faith for every believer. Worship must be alive, inspired by the love of God and productive of right action (ihsan).

1. Bearing witness that there is no God but God and that Muhammad (pbuh) is the messenger of God (Shahada)
2. Performing prayers (salat) five times a day.
3. Giving Zakat (almsgiving in service of the needy)- for those able to afford it.
4. Fasting Ramadan-annual fast during month of Ramadan for those able.
5. Performing Hajj-pilgrimage at least once a lifetime for those able.

Madhhabs:

(lit. 'ways') these are the 4 main systems (or 'ways') for implementing shari'ah and hence the laws of the Qur'an and Sunnah in everyday life. They are based on the work and authority of expert scholars. Some are stricter than others.

The two most important practical virtues/values in Islam are:

Taqwa = God consciousness/piety - ensuring that all our thoughts, words and actions are in accordance with the Divine Will.

Hilm = Forbearance, forgiveness, humility in all our dealings with fellow humans.

Historical events in the early days of Islam following the death of Prophet Muhammad (pbuh) led to the development of two main groupings in the Islamic world:

1. **Sunni** (followers of the Sunnah): approx 80%.
2. **Shi'ah**: approx 20%: followers of the tradition of Ali, Muhammad's nephew and son-in-law and closest companion.

Shi'ah Muslims reject the Sunni collections of sunnah and hadith as being inauthentic/unreliable and have their own collection traced back to Ali (the nephew and son-in-law of the Prophet Muhammad pbuh) and his followers. Shi'ah Muslims have experienced persecution as minorities living in Sunni Muslim states.

Annual events relating to Faith:

The Muslim calendar is lunar, with each year composed of 12 months of twenty- nine or thirty days. It is eleven days shorter than a solar year and dates will vary to solar calendar. The start of new month is dependent on sighting of the new moon. This means, for example, that Ramadan occurs a couple of weeks earlier each solar year.

Event:	Date:	Significance:
Ramadan	9th month of Islamic calendar	Worshippers refrain from food, drink, and sexual intercourse from sunrise to sunset. It is a time of immense blessings and Spiritual devotion. Abstentions reflect devotion to God, as a person abstains for God alone. Also, increases self-discipline, patience, decreases selfishness and tends to a sense of unity between Muslims and equality before God. Children and those who are ill are exempt. Also, women who are menstruating, breastfeeding or post-natal bleeding are also exempt from the fast.
Lailat al Qadr	One of the last 10 days of (Night of Power) Ramadan, generally the 27th	Marks the time when revelations of the Qur'an commenced and the first few verses were revealed to Prophet Muhammad (pbuh) during the last third of Ramadan. The process continued for 23 years.
Id ul Fitr (day of feast)	(end of Ramadan)	A day of festivities, which marks the end of Ramadan and begins with communal thanks-giving prayer in the mosque.
Id ul Adha (day of sacrifice)	10th day of month Dhu'l Hijah, the 12th month of the year	Three-day celebration marking the end of Hajj. Commemorates the sacrifice and submission exhibited by Abraham and his son Ishmael. Muslim families who can afford it sacrifice an animal as Abraham did in substitution for his son. Meat is distributed to poor and one's family.

Daily acts of Faith/Devotion:

Prayer is the most fundamental act of worship and is performed five times daily: dawn, midday, late afternoon, sunset, late evening. Prayer is the linking up with the Divine to keep ensuring that all one's day, actions and thoughts are regulated and in tune with the Divine Will.

Prayer is obligatory from puberty onwards except for women who are menstruating or postnatal bleeding.

Ritual Cleansing (*wudu*) must take place prior to all prayers and is seen as the key to unlocking the benefits of prayer and is an act of worship in itself. This includes washing face, arms, hair and feet. During prayer Muslims face the qiblah, the direction of the Kaaba (a cube construction of stone and mortar, generally regarded as the first place of worship of the One God), in Makka.

Wudu is a spiritual cleansing and the believer should be clean in a physical sense even before doing wudu. A thorough morning wudu can last through to the next prayer time so long as it is not broken.

Acts which break wudu purity include:
Going to the toilet; touching genitals and posterior; falling asleep; getting dirty; contact with bodily fluids of animals (e.g. a dog's saliva).

For some schools of Islamic law, contact with a woman or man whom one can potentially marry, would also constitute breaking of wudu.

If no running water is available, a 'dry ablution' can be performed.

Non-obligatory acts of worship include voluntary fasts, reciting the Qur'an and seeking knowledge. Any mundane act made with the intention of pleasing God becomes sacred, an act of worship (ibadah).

Weekly acts of Faith:

Jummah prayers- Friday is a holy day, full of blessing and commences (as do all days) on sunset Thursday. It is mandatory for men to attend congregational prayer. Prayer takes place of usual midday prayer and is accompanied by two sermons and almsgiving.

Worshippers resume their usual affairs once prayer is concluded.

Food:

Muslims are religiously forbidden to eat pork (and all products of pigs), consuming alcohol or any form of intoxicant. Muslims can eat poultry, mutton and beef, but they must be slaughtered according to Islamic law.

It is recommended and is normal practice to eat food with the right hand.

The left hand may be used for any polluting tasks (e.g. toilet). This is good practice for avoiding infections.

Fasting (abstaining from food or drink) takes place during the month of Ramadan for 30 days from sunrise to sunset.

Greetings:

As Salamu Alaikum (wa Rahmatulla wa Barakatu)- 'Peace and Blessing of God be upon you' ('and the mercy and grace of God')

REPLY: *Wa Alaikum Salam* - 'And Peace be with you also'

Always shake with right hand (left hand can be polluting).

Dress:

Modesty and respect are the key. Both men and women are obliged to cover their bodies although there is no specific form of dress. Women cover hair and their body, except hands and face. Men are obliged to cover from their naval to knees, however, modesty necessitates that they cover their bodies. Men are recommended to imitate the dress of the Prophet. Modesty is part of Iman (Islamic faith).

Bathing and showers: Islamic modesty precludes even same sex bathing and showering in the nude. This is an important consideration with respect to provision of bathing and showering facilities and practices in all sorts of institutions including schools, sports centres, armed forces, hostels and hotels, etc.

Speech:

Words that denigrate the Creator, any of His Prophets are a gross insult.

Sending peace and blessing on the Prophet Muhammad (pbuh = Peace be upon him) when his name is mentioned is very common and can be seen as a sign of piety. This is also true of other Prophets.

Inshallah = 'God willing' is commonly uttered whenever speaking about future events.

Al hamdulillah = 'God be praised' is commonly uttered after mentioning something good.

Religious Symbols/Imagery:

None are used in worship. Images of people and animals are prohibited in mosques for fear of committing idolatry. However, it is popular practice to wear inscriptions of Qur'anic verses on bracelets and pendants (e.g. the famous *ayat al kursi* = 'verse of the throne').

Calligraphy (elaborate inscriptions of Qur'anic verses) and geometric patterns (symbolising the unity of God that underlies all the complexity of creation) are popular decorations in homes and Mosques. The crescent moon and star is the most widespread symbol of Islam and represents the light and guidance that the faith gives to believers, but it is not used as a religious symbol in worship.

Gender Issues:

Women have equal spiritual status in Islam, though Islamic law may differentiate according to what are believed to be differences in the divinely given nature and social roles of male and female. Women are not obliged to go to the Mosque to pray. Direct contact between unrelated men and women is avoided, unless necessary. When visiting a Muslim home, a female on her own should not invite any non-related males into the home. Outside marriage and close family, men and women should avoid being alone together.

In a caring or hospital situation, it is usually preferable to have carers of the same sex, especially when physical contact cannot be avoided. However, it is important to remember that practices and interpretations of Islamic Law vary greatly according to culture, but certain core values are accepted by all.

Visiting Place of Worship:

Principles of respect and modesty apply. The **Mosque/Masjid** (lit. = 'place of prostration') is open every day as all five prayers are performed at mosque and all men are expected to attend.

All visitors should remove shoes, as the carpeted area is a place of prayer.

Seating is generally on the floor, unless not possible. Visitors should dress modestly and covering hair for women is an important sign of respect.

Women are separated from men: usually in a women's gallery or else placed behind the men.

Mosques are built orientated toward **Makka**. Mandatory elements are an indication of the direction of prayer (the direction of Makka is called *Qiblah*) by the construction of the mihrab, which is a niche in the wall. Many mosques contain a *minbar*, which is a pulpit from which the Imam gives the obligatory sermon on the Friday communal prayer.

Visiting the Home:

Remember principles of cleanliness and respect. It is common practice to remove shoes (they can bring in dirt into home). Avoid touching members of opposite sex. Washing dishes is normally done under running water. Many Muslims do not use toilet paper, or do not regard the use of toilet paper as sufficient, because it is not the most efficient way of removing stains. The use of running water from a jug or shower is a preferred and more efficient method for removing impurities.

Respect for elders is a key religious virtue.

Hospitality is a great spiritual virtue and it is polite to accept what is offered.

Imam: an Imam can be any righteous person learned in the Qur'an who is well respected and can command the respect of the community. There is no priesthood in Islam, but there are learned scholars, the *ulamah*, who can command a great deal of authority and are regularly consulted on how to apply Qur'anic teachings to every day life.

Death:

Apply principles of respect, dignity and modesty. Death is seen as the beginning of real life, i. e. the eternal life. It is paramount that the body is cleansed, bathed, shrouded in an unstitched white shroud and buried as soon as possible (within three days or less). The grave is commonly dug in an L-shape and the body is placed it so it faces Makka. Cremation is not Islamic practice.

For most Muslims, it is important that the family or respected members of the Muslim community handle the body and cleanse and shroud it. Final washing of the body before being placed in the shroud should be done by Muslims as prayers are constantly recited during this process.

Event Planning:

Avoid Fridays between 12.00 and 3.00pm (some would argue that Fridays should be avoided altogether).

Avoid festivals so that Muslims may be allowed to celebrate with relatives and friends.

Ramadan: Remember that during the whole month of Ramadan (which moves relative to the solar calendar) the Muslim community is fasting in daylight hours. It is a very special time of community spirit, inner reflection, intense prayer and piety. Towards sunset the community likes to gather together with family and friends at home or the mosques to break the fast and pray together. Therefore avoid event times that may impinge on this. Ramadan also involves waking up early before sunrise to have a meal and drink: this can be a tiring time (especially for mothers!).

Ensure that prayer facilities are available, including clean washing facilities for ablutions before prayer and eating. Cater for food needs: provide Halal meat (and clearly label it) if possible. If this is not possible, then ensure that vegetarian options are available (and clearly labelled).

Sensitivity and respect for the Islamic prohibition on alcohol should be shown.

Showers may be regarded as more preferable than baths (washing with running water that carries away dirt is considered cleaner and more effective than a bath). Shower and bathing facilities should accommodate Islamic values of modesty.

GENERAL FAITH HEALTH WARNING:

- A little knowledge can be very dangerous!
- Treat all people of a faith as individuals and beware of generalisations.
- Be aware that there is a great diversity of belief and practise within each faith.
- Ask 'What do you do?' NOT 'Why do you do it?' Don't expect people to know and have to explain/justify WHY they do something.
- Always treat objects held to be sacred with great respect: e.g. holy books, sacred pictures, special items of clothing and jewellery, prayer beads, food and incense that may have a sacred value for the person.

Liverpool's Muslim Community and Heritage

Liverpool is blessed with a great Muslim heritage and boasts the oldest Muslim community in Britain and Britain's first established Mosque.

The leader of the first British community of Muslims, Abdullah Quilliam, was born in Liverpool in 1856. He was a descendant of Captain John Quilliam R.N. who sailed on HMS Victory with Nelson. Educated at the Liverpool Institute, he travelled to Morocco in 1882-3, where he became interested in Islam. In 1887, aged 31 he proclaimed himself to be Muslim. In 1887 he gave a lecture at the Temperance League in Mount Vernon Street, where he started to hold weekly meetings. Mrs Cates, later Fatima Cates, was the first convert in Liverpool after himself.

In 1889, the group moved to Brougham Terrace in West Derby Road. In 1893, they began to publish *The Crescent* weekly and *The Islamic World* monthly. Both were distributed to 20 countries worldwide. The Liverpool Muslim Institute numbered approx. 150 people by the turn of the century.

At their centre at 8 Brougham Terrace, open house was kept for both Muslims and non-Muslims alike. A boarding school for boys and a day school for girls were established. There was a library, reading room, museum and science lab. Classes were held in a wide variety of subjects. Men and women played an equal and active role.

In 1896, they bought 66 and 68 Sheil Road, which became a children's home for orphaned children or for children of parents who were unable to support them. The home was called the Medina home for children. Over the years, the group received abuse both verbal and physical. A local Sunday School teacher was arrested for throwing a piece of rock hidden in a snowball at the Muezzin as he stood at one of the upper windows of 8 Brougham Terrace, calling the Muslims to prayer. A group of English Muslim ladies had mud thrown at them as they left the building.

In 1908, Sheikh Abdullah left Liverpool and went to Turkey. The buildings were vacated and the group dispersed. In April 1932, Sheikh Abdullah died.

There are about 15,000 Muslims in Liverpool gathered under one society, which is called the Liverpool Muslim Society. There is one main Mosque in Liverpool, the Al Rahma Mosque on Hatherley/ Mulgrave Street, Liverpool 8. The second, much smaller, is at 8 Cramond Avenue, Liverpool 18.

There has been a Muslim presence in Britain for at least 300 years. The East India Company recruited seamen from Yemen, Gujarat, Sind, Assam and Bengal, known by the British as Lascars, and a number of these created small settlements in port towns and cities in Britain, including Liverpool.

Following the opening of the Suez Canal in 1869, seamen originally from Yemen settled in small communities in Cardiff, Liverpool, London, South Shields and Tyneside and set up zawiyahs (small mosques or prayer rooms).

The first Mosque (after Brougham Terrace) was established by a member of the Yemeni community, Haji Ali Hazzan, in a terrace house on St James Street (in front of the Anglican Cathedral). He also formed the Liverpool Muslim Society in 1953. Liverpool has a long-established Somali community, which has grown considerably in recent decades. Liverpool's Asian Muslim community also has a long heritage. Some of the first Muslim Asians to come to Liverpool arrived in the 1920s and 1930's, earning a living as peddlers, traders and entertainers. In 1965 the foundation stone was laid for the Al Rahma Mosque. A temporary mosque was established in a house on Kimberley St (Liverpool 8) whilst the main mosque was being constructed. With the growth of the Muslim community, in 1979 additional space added to the Al Rahma mosque. It can now accommodate over 1000 Muslims. In recent decades, the Muslim community in Liverpool has continued to expand in numbers and national heritages, including Turkish, Malaysian, Sudanese, Kosovan, Bosnian and Kurdish. However, Liverpool's old tradition of conversion (or 'reversion') to Islam has also continued and Liverpool-born Black and Liverpool-born White members form an essential part of this unique community.

There are well-established education and welfare systems in place and there are many cultural organisations. There is an Islamic Institute that has premises on Cramond Avenue (purchased in 2000) and provides regular Friday (Jummah) prayers for the growing Muslim community in the South of Liverpool.

The Institute could now be said to constitute Liverpool's second Mosque and is presently undergoing extension works. The Institute offers courses in Qur'anic studies for both children and adults.

In 1995 an Islamic Resource Centre was opened called 'The Olive Tree', on Renshaw Street. The Al-Ghazali Centre on Earle Road offers educational support, classes, training, etc within an Islamic multi-cultural ethos.

Kingsley Road Primary School, L8, was opened as Liverpool's first school with an Islamic Ethos. The new building contains ablution rooms and a hall adapted for Islamic prayer - including a Mihrab indicating the qiblah (direction of Mecca).

The Abdullah Quilliam Society has developed an excellent proposal to create an Abdullah Quilliam Heritage Centre at the old Brougham Terrace site. It would become a centre of Islamic studies, education and culture.

Thanks and acknowledgements to:

Brother Akbar Ali:	Islamic Institute and Merseyside Council of Faiths
Sister Sahra Ahmed:	Al Ghazali Centre (and Liverpool Community Spirit)
Sister Somaia McTeer:	Abdullah Quilliam Society and Manager, the Olive Tree

THE RASTAFARIAN COMMUNITY

Faith: **Rastafarian** (from 'Ras Tafari' = 'Prince Tafari' the name of Emperor Haile Selassie I of Ethiopia)
Faith Community: **Rastafarian**

Holy Books/Scriptures:

The Holy Bible. Another very important source of tradition is the Kebra Nagast - the ancient Ethiopian Orthodox Church writing that recounts the story of the descent of the Ethiopian Royal line from Solomon and the Queen of Sheba and the movement of the Ark of the Covenant to Ethiopia.

Core Belief:

The Rastafarian faith is rooted in Christianity and Judaism and the experiences of slavery and alienation of the Black African Diaspora people in Jamaica and beyond.

In the early 19th century, the Black political and spiritual leader, Marcus Garvey, on the basis of his reading of the Bible and particular scriptures such as Psalm 89 (which says that God will provide good kings to guide people throughout history), predicted that a great king would be crowned in Africa who would unite the Black peoples and bring them hope and freedom after centuries of slavery and oppression (*"Look to Africa for the crowning of a Black King, he shall be the Redeemer"*).

Soon afterwards Ras Tafari ('Head Creator') was crowned **Haile Selassie** ('Glory of the Trinity'), King of Ethiopia. People in Jamaica began to see Haile Selassie as the fulfilment of Marcus Garvey's prophecy and as a source of political and spiritual salvation.

Rastafarians followed the teaching of the Ethiopian Orthodox Church that the Ethiopian Royal family were direct descendents of Solomon and hence King David (the messianic 'family root/branch of David').

For Rastafarians, rooted in Christian tradition, the messianic associations of this line became more and more significant. For most Rastafarians, Haile Selassie became seen as a messianic figure who embodied the teachings of spiritual and political **liberation** and salvation from oppression. Calling themselves **Rastafarians** (followers of the Ras Tafari), this new movement gained popularity in Jamaica. The influence of the Ethiopian Orthodox Church can also be seen in the Rastafarian emphasis upon obedience to many of the Old Testament Laws of Leviticus (such as the Nazarite vow of not cutting hair and also, following many of the Sabbath regulations, including keeping Sabbath on a Saturday).

Also, at birth, each Rastafarian becomes a member of one of the 12 Tribes of Israel (and may be given the appropriate tribal name) according to the following system:

TRIBE	MONTH	COLOUR
Reuben	April	Silver
Simeon	May	Gold
Levi	June	Purple
Judah	July	Brown
Issacher	August	Yellow
Zebulon	September	Pink
Dan	October	Blue
Gad	November	Red
Asher	December	Grey
Naphtali	January	Green
Joseph	February	White
Benjamin	March	Black

However, it is the experiences and the legacy of **slavery** and oppression that made the Old Testament Scriptures such as the Psalms, Exodus and the Prophets particularly appealing and relevant to the Black community in Jamaica and much of the African Diaspora world-wide.

As with the Psalms, the message of hope and liberation was often most powerfully and soulfully expressed through music. Rastafarians such as Bob Marley fused traditional African and contemporary West Indian musical forms, resulting in the world-wide spread and the appeal of Reggae music.

Rastafarianism has spread world-wide and even has many non-Black converts. It is estimated that there may now be several million followers.

Rastafarians may smoke marijuana, regarded as a natural God-given herb sanctioned in the Bible in Psalm 104:14. Rastafarians believe that the spirit or presence of Jah (God) resides in each individual. It is common to use the term 'I' to refer to this presence.

Greetings:

Rastafarians may 'hail' each other by saying *Greetings, Hail Ras*, or *Rasta fari*. Other common greetings are *Peace and Love* or *One Love*.

Sacred Language:
There is no official sacred language. However, Amharic, an ancient Ethiopian language is held in great respect. Jamaican patois is prevalent as is the traditional English of the King James Bible. God is often referred to as '**Jah**' (derived from the English attempt at uttering the unutterable sacred name of God revealed in the Old Testament).

Sacred Land:
Ethiopia is a sacred land to most Rastafarians and may often be referred to by using the term 'Zion' (a Hebrew term for Jerusalem). Within Ethiopia *Shashamane* is a Holy place because it is the land given by Emperor Haile Selassie to the people of the African Diaspora.

Annual events relating to Faith:
Many, if not most Rastafarians follow the traditional Christian festivals and celebrations of Lent, Easter, Pentecost and Epiphany (see section on Christianity). Also:
- 8th January: Ethiopian Christmas.
- 23rd July: Birthday of His Imperial Majesty Emperor Haile Selassie.
- 17th August: Birthday of Marcus Garvey.
- 2nd November: The Coronation of HIM Haile Selassie.

Daily acts of Faith/Devotion:
These include regular prayer, reading of Holy Scripture and singing praises to God.

Communal Acts of Worship:
Rastafarians often meet on a weekly basis in a local home or community centre for worship and discussion. *Nyabinghi* (a term derived from a secret African society that met in the Congo and Rwanda during the late 19th century) is the name often given to regular gatherings of Rastafarians for worship. Drumming and singing Jah's (God's) praises are common as is 'Reasoning', the term given to the exchange of ideas, teachings, spiritual guidance and passing on of other oral traditions.

Structure:
Rastafarians are divided into different groups including:
The Nyabinghi Order.
The Twelve Tribes of Israel: Recognise the divinity of Haile Selassie, but are closer to Orthodox Christianity and welcome people of all descent as Rasta.
The Ethiopian World Federation: recognise the Divinity of Haile Selassie and tend only to accept those of African descent as true Rastas.
Bobo Dread: Follow very strict codes (e.g. always cover heads with white turban) and follow the teachings of the prophet Emmanuel.

Food:
Rastafarians place emphasis upon living a healthy, natural or 'I-tal' lifestyle, a major component of which is eating healthy 'I-tal' foods, grown organically if possible. Many Rastafarians follow a vegetarian diet and most avoid pork and the flesh of other scavengers such as shellfish. Alcohol is also discouraged. Stricter Rastafarians may avoid the consumption of all stimulants including tea and coffee.

Dress:
Many Rastafarians follow the Old Testament Nazarite practice of not cutting the hair and growing long locks, often called Dreadlocks because they embody Dread or Fear/Awe of the Almighty Jah.
Many women dress according to codes of modesty and may often cover the head and wear long dresses as opposed to trousers.
Men may wear a knitted or leather Tam - a hat.
The symbolically important colours of Red Gold and Green are often worn.

Symbols:
Commonly used symbols are the **Royal Flag of Ethiopia (Red Gold and Green)** with/and the **Lion of Judah** symbolising the descent of Haile Selassie.
The Star of David is frequently used for the same reason. Rastafarians commonly use a hand gesture of placing the thumbs and first fingers of each hand together (in imitation of the gestures used by the Emperor Haile Selassie) which is seen as representing the Holy Trinity and unity, but also peace and war (the heart and the spear).

Visiting Homes:
Principles of respect and cleanliness apply. Many Rastafarian households prefer the removal of shoes before entering.

Gender Issues:
Many Rastafarians have a more traditional approach to the role and status of males and females in which the male is regarded as the natural head. However, practices vary widely.

Death:
The words Death and Dead may be considered negative and replaced with 'Passing' or 'Passed'. Life on earth is seen by many as a preparation for the eternal life.

GENERAL FAITH HEALTH WARNING:

- A little knowledge can be very dangerous!
- Treat all people of a faith as **individuals** and beware of generalisations.
- Be aware that there is a great diversity of belief and practise within each faith.
- Ask 'What do you do?' NOT 'Why do you do it?' Don't expect people to know and have to explain/justify WHY they do something.
- Always treat objects held to be sacred with great respect: e.g. holy books, sacred pictures, special items of clothing and jewellery, prayer beads, food and incense that may have a sacred value for the person.

Liverpool's Rastafarian Heritage and Community

There are estimated to be over 100 practising Rastafarians in Liverpool (and about 100,000 in the UK). The Liverpool community traces its origins back to 1970. There is no Rastafarian centre in the city (individuals may travel to Manchester for communal meetings).

H.I.M. Haile Selassie visited Liverpool on a number of occasions and stayed at the Adelphi Hotel.

His son and successor, Crown Prince Asfa Wossen, later H.I.M. Emperor Amha Selassie Ist, resided in Liverpool (in Waverley Road) whilst studying for his degree in Political Science and Public Administration at the University of Liverpool.

Thanks and acknowledgements to:

Erroll Graham: *Liverpool Community Spirit and Liverpool Faith Network*

Levi Tafari: *Urban Griot (and Liverpool Community Spirit)*

THE SIKH COMMUNITY

Faith: **Sikhism**
Faith Community: **Sikh** (= 'follower, disciple, learner')

Holy Books/Scriptures:

The Guru Granth Sahib is a title of honour for the final collection of Sikh Holy scriptures. The earlier collection was known as *Adi Granth* ('first collection'). They are written in the Gurmurkhi script. They contain writings and sayings of the Gurus and important Hindu and Muslim saints. The Adi Granth is treated as a living Guru and hence with utmost respect: e.g. covered in beautiful cloths (*Rumalla*), placed under ornate canopies, waved over with an ornate fan (*chauri*) placed in regal bedroom at nighttimes. Before touching/reading the scriptures, Sikhs should wash. They form the sacred core of all Sikh worship and rituals.

In the marriage ceremony, the bride and groom must walk around the Adi Granth four times. In the naming ceremony for a new-born child, the scripture is opened at random and the first word of the verse at the top left-hand page is read and the name chosen must begin with one of the letters of the word.

Sacred Languages:

The Holy Scriptures are written in *Gurmurkhi* ('The Mouth of the Guru') - a written form of Punjabi.

Core Belief:

Sikhism is rooted in the teachings of the ten Gurus, the first of which was Guru Nanak Dev (1469-1539), who was born at Talwandi in the Punjab. At the age of around thirty, he received a call to preach the Word of God. His message emphasised the **Oneness** of God and the importance of honesty and integrity in the practice of any religion. The community that he founded became known as the community of 'Sikhs', meaning 'disciples', or 'learners'. In 1699, the tenth Guru, Guru Gobind Singh, instituted Amrit Ceremony, which initiates Sikhs into the **Khalsa Panth**: the community of initiated Sikhs, whose identity is marked out by the so-called **Five 'K's** (see section on Dress below). The spiritual centre of the Sikh faith and community is the Golden Temple in Amritsar, Punjab, India.

Sikh's believe in the Oneness of God, the Almighty Creator, who is Truth. God reveals His will to mankind through the teachings of his chosen teachers, the **Gurus**. All humans contain a spark of the Divine nature given to them by God. It is our duty to struggle to follow God's will by following the guidance He has given through the Gurus. Humans are re-born according to their use of their God-given free-will. This process of re-birth can be stopped and liberation, bliss and happiness achieved, through replacing all of our worldly desires with service and devotion to God.

Humans should serve God through worship and through living their life according to four central Principles:

i   Reciting God's name
ii Earning a living through honest work in the community
iii Sharing any material wealth with those in need
iv Active community service

Annual events relating to Faith:

Event:	Date:	Significance:
Baisakhi	April	Anniversary of the day (in 1699) Guru Gobind Singh founded the order of the Khalsa. The Sikh flag outside the Gurdwara is replaced. Prayer and kirtan (hymns) are offered and the story regarding the event is remembered and celebrated.
Martyrdom of Guru Arjan	May/June	Celebration of Guru Arjan who completed the first collection of scriptures - the Adi Granth and was killed by the Muslim Mughal Emperor and became the first Martyr Guru of the Sikhs.
Diwali	October/November	Celebrates the victory of the sixth Guru, Hargobind, who delivered fifty-two Hindu kings from the imprisonment by the Mughal Emperor Auranzeb. Marked with bonfires and fireworks as well as prayer and kirtan (hymns).
Guru Nanak's Birthday	Oct/November	Three-day celebration of the birth of the founder of the Sikh faith.
Martyrdom of Guru Tgh Bahadur	December	Celebration of the martyrdom of the ninth Guru.
Birthday of Guru Gobind Singh	Dec/January	Birthday of the tenth Guru and founder of the Khalsa.

Holy Place:
The Golden Temple of Amritsar in Punjab.

Daily acts of Faith/Devotion:
In the morning Sikhs would wake early, bathe/shower and meditate on One God before saying morning prayers *(Jap)*. In the evening, the *Sodar Rehras* is recited, before going to bed the *Sohila* is recited.

The most important and commonly recited Sikh prayer is the **Mool Mantra**, which is said to contain the essence of the Sikh faith:

"There is but One God, the Eternal Truth, the Creator, without fear, without enmity, timeless, immanent, beyond birth and death, self-existent: by the grace of the Guru, made known."

Weekly acts of Faith:
There is no single holy day of the week. In the UK, for convenience' sake, the Gurdwara is usually visited for Sadh Sangrat (= holy congregational worship) on Saturdays or Sundays. In Liverpool, the Sikh Community Centre holds its main service on a Sunday and is honoured to welcome guests from all faith communities to take part in both the service and, of course, the langha (the meal).

Food:
Dietary restrictions vary for Sikhs. The only explicit prohibition regarding food is eating Halal meat (killed according to the Muslim rite). Amongst non-vegetarians, very few eat beef (as the cow is regarded as a sacred animal in Indian culture). Some Sikhs are vegetarian. Food is a matter of individual conscience and it is worth discussing with each individual Sikh what his or her requirements are. Food is traditionally eaten with the right hand.

Sikhs are encouraged to avoid smoking and consuming alcohol.

Names: All Sikh men are given the name **Singh** - Lion. All Sikh women are given the name **Kaur** - Princess. Sikhs often give their first name and the title Kaur or Singh, but family names can be requested.

Greetings:
Sat Siri Akal = 'God is Eternal Truth'.

Dress:
Principles of modesty and dignity apply. Women are encouraged to dress modestly and cover their bodies and often wear the *Kirpan* - knife - in a miniature or symbolic form). Men are encouraged to wear the Five 'K's, which are the five signs for being a member of the Sikh Khalsa (= the 'pure' community of Sikhs). These are:

1 **Kesh**: uncut hair: Symbolizes the nobility of our natural God-given state
2 **Khanga**: comb (symbol of self-discipline and cleanliness)
3. **Kara**: steel bangle: worn on right wrist as reminder of maintaining God-consciousness in all actions.
4 **Kirpan**: double-edged ceremonial sword symbolising the struggle against injustice in oneself and the world. (kirpa = kindness; An = protecting honour).
5 **Kachera**: boxer shorts: symbol of chastity and self-control.

Removal of the turban and touching of the head by another person is a major insult and should be avoided unless absolutely necessary.

Jewellery is popular and carers should always seek permission before having to remove any items of jewellery that may have a sacred value/symbolism.

In caring institutions and hospitals, care should be taken to always seek permission before cutting a Sikh client's hair.

Speech:
Elders and women command special courtesy respect from younger members and the community.

Religious Symbols/Imagery:
The two most commonly used Sikh symbols and images are:

1 **Khanda**: The symbol of the Sikh faith and community, which is also placed on an orange flag and flown outside every Sikh Gurdwara. It comprises:
   i Two crossed swords representing the (struggle to fulfil God's Will in the) two realms of existence - the Spiritual and the temporal/political.
   ii A central, double-edged sword - representing the Oneness, Truth and Strength of God
   iii The Outer circle - representing God's eternity.

2 **Ek Onkar**: The phrase, 'God is One', written in Gurumurkhi script.

It is also very common for temples and homes to be decorated with pictures of the Gurus.

Visiting Place of Worship:
Apply general principles of cleanliness, modesty and respect. Men and women sit in the same room, but on different sides. Remove shoes and cover heads.

The place of worship is called the **Gurdwara** (House of the Guru). The Holy Guru Granth Sahib, (the Sikh Holy Scripture) is placed on a raised platform with a canopy and is highly venerated and is regarded as the living embodiment of the Ten Sikh Gurus. The devotee bows down to pay respect on entering the prayer room, observing silence while recitation takes place.

Sikhs do not turn their backs on the platform containing the Holy scriptures. Visitors should show their respect by avoiding this also.

Hospitality and food play a very central role and on Sundays when the congregation meet together. An essential part of Sikh religious activity is the **Langha** - the communal meal, which represents an act of hospitality (a sacred duty in the Sikh faith). All visitors are invited to attend and in particular non-Sikhs are welcomed to share. It is polite and also respectful to accept the generous offer of hospitality. Modest and smart clothing should be worn when visiting the temple.

Visiting the Home:
Principles of cleanliness and respect apply. It may be traditional to remove shoes. Use the right hand for touching food (avoid use of left hand). Always show great respect to elders.

Death:
Principles of respect, dignity and protection apply. The dying may receive comfort from hearing hymns from the Guru Granth Sahib. It is common for family members to wish to handle and lay out the dead. Men are wrapped in a white cotton shroud with a turban. Older women are wrapped in a white shroud and young women in a red shroud. Sikhs do not bury their deceased. Cremation takes place. Religious service is held and hymns are recited from the Holy Guru Granth Sahib.

Gender Issues:
Women and men are considered equal in the Sikh faith. Guru Nanak, the founder of the Sikh faith granted women equal status by saying 'How can you call a woman inferior when it is her who gives birth to saints and princes and without her the whole race would be extinct'.
In a caring or hospital situation, it is usually preferable to have carers of the same sex, especially when physical contact cannot be avoided.

Priests:
A priest is a person who is learned in the Sikh scriptures (Guru Granth Sahib) and can recite them and also the devotional songs that form an essential part of Sikh worship. In recent times, the Sikh community has established training colleges inside India where the candidates complete a two year course (in Sikh scriptures, song and history).

Priests are not essential for ceremonies if there is someone who can recite the appropriate scriptures and sing the necessary songs (e.g. marriage - sing 4 hymns called Lavan; death - recite the *Kirtan Sohila* - prayer recited by all Sikhs when retiring to bed each night).

Event Planning:
Avoid major festivals and Sundays.
Check out food requirements and clearly label (especially any Halal/Kosher food).
Accommodate prayer times.
Showers may be regarded as more preferable than baths (washing with running water that carries away dirt is considered cleaner and more effective than a bath).

GENERAL FAITH HEALTH WARNING:

- A little knowledge can be very dangerous!
- Treat all people of a faith as **individuals** and beware of generalisations.
- Be aware that there is a great diversity of belief and practise within each faith..
- Ask 'What do you do?' NOT 'Why do you do it?' Don't expect people to know and have to explain/justify WHY they do something.
- Always treat objects held to be sacred with great respect: e.g. holy books, sacred pictures, special items of clothing and jewellery, prayer beads, food and incense that may have a sacred value for the person.

Liverpool's Sikh Community and Heritage

Sikhs were probably amongst the first individuals to come to Liverpool from the Indian sub-continent as traders in the 1920s and 1930s, though they may have accompanied the earliest settlers who came to Liverpool in the 1850s. However, it was after the Indian Independence in 1947 that the first Sikh families settled in Liverpool. In December 1965, Mr H.S. Sohal, who had come to Liverpool to teach, met a Sikh man, Mr Panesar, who lived in number 8 Berkeley Street (a grand Georgian terrace recently demolished) Liverpool 8. He offered the attic in his house for a meeting place. Sikhs used this for worship and meetings until 1975. Members of the Sikh community also met in a house they purchased in Newstead Street, Liverpool 8 (now also demolished).

The founding members of the United Sikh Association and the Gurdwara on Wellington Avenue were Mr H.S. Sohal, Mr I.S. Khanijau, Mr B.S. Panesar, Mr G.S. Khanijau and Mr K.S. Hansra.

In 1976, when the Hindu community moved to their present site on Edge Lane, Mr Sohal, Mr G.S Khanijau and the late Dr D.P. Singh took a bank loan to purchase the Lord Krishna Temple building on Botanic Road for the Sikh community and used it as the Guru Nanak Temple.

After a fire in 1979, the Sikh community remained without a place to meet and carry out any corporate religious, social and cultural activity for three years.

On advice and guidance from Mr Nigel Mellor, Community Liaison Officer, Liverpool City Council, Mr Sohal pursued the matter to obtain a grant from the Urban Aid Fund to establish a Sikh community Centre in the Old Methodist Church building (Wellington Avenue) in July 1983. Through patience and perseverance, they accomplished the present two-story building in 1994 to meet all the needs of the community. Liverpool's Sikhs work in many different professions including medicine, computing, engineering, groceries, and teaching. The Cains brewery, part of the biggest family owned brewery in Europe is owned by a Liverpool Sikh family the Dusanj.

There are an estimated 500 Sikhs in Liverpool, up to 500,000 in the UK and approximately 21 million Sikhs worldwide.

Thanks and acknowledgements to:

Mr H.S. Sohal: United Sikh Association
Mr Sardar Singh: Liverpool Community Spirit

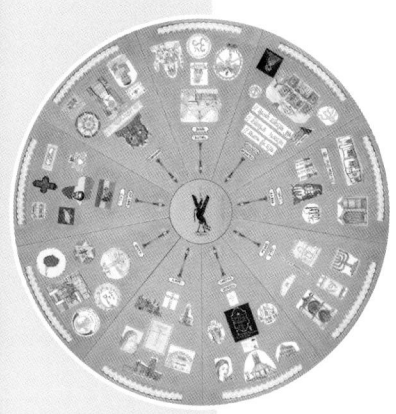

LIVERPOOL COMMUNITY SPIRIT (LCS) THE ROUND TABLE OF FAITHS

Oh what a good and joyful thing it is when brethren dwell together in Unity

Aims:

To construct a round table representing the unity in diversity of Liverpool's diverse faith communities. Thereby, to promote:

- inter-faith awareness, understanding, cohesion and co-operation
- awareness of, pride in and active concern to preserve and enhance Liverpool's uniquely rich heritage of diverse faith communities.

To develop the Table into a teaching resource for both the LCS Adult Learner's courses on Faith diversity and also (in partnership with Hope University P.G.C.E. Department) for Religious Education and Citizenship Education in Liverpool's Schools.

Process:

The images were drawn by:
  i   Local Liverpool school children as a product of Liverpool Community Spirit workshops exploring Liverpool's diverse faith heritage.
  ii Young people from the diverse faith communities.
  iii Members of Liverpool Community Spirit Youth Council (14-19 yr olds from inner-city Liverpool who devise and deliver innovative citizenship and inter-faith projects in their local neighbourhoods in order to promote unity, social cohesion, inclusion, community sustainability and inclusive, active community spirit in their local neighbourhoods.

A competition was held and the top 12 drawings were picked out by an independent judge (Vinnie Cleghorne - a local Liverpool 8 artist) and each artist rewarded with a gift voucher and an LCS certificate signed by the Chair of the Merseyside Council of Faiths and the LCS Co-ordinator.
All the images were fixed onto the nine table panels by the traditional process of decoupage (using over 90 layers of varnish) undertaken by the British Guild of Decoupeurs.
The table panels, base and legs constructed by Liverpool Cathedral craftsmen.
The table was sponsored by the generous support of Miltons the Jewellers; the Community Chest Fund and the Westhill Endowment Trust.

Content:

Each panel represents drawings of items from a major Liverpool faith community including:
  i   Drawings of buildings associated with the faith community in Liverpool
  ii Faith symbols
  iii A Liverpool 'road sign' with a community value chosen by each Faith community
  iv A Mersey Tunnel lamp (from the Liverpool Architect, Rowse's 1930's designs for the first Mersey Tunnel): symbolising the light that each faith community and its chosen community value shines out and illuminates the Liverpool Community
  v   Waves representing the sea of Faith and the River Mersey that unites us all in one community

Each of the Road signs has a red letter, which combined together, makeup the word 'Liverpool', representing our united community spirit, community values and our unity in diversity.

Guide to the Individual Panel images:

PANEL L Christian Community 1

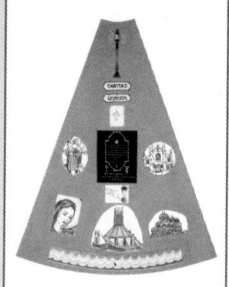

1. CARITAS (Latin) and AGAPE (Greek) - LOVE - central community value
2. Crucifix - Christ crucified - the heart of the Christian Faith
3. St Anthony patron Saint of St Anthony's Church, Scotland Road
4. Plaque marking the spot, where, in 432 AD, St Patrick preached before going to Ireland, located in Marybone, L3
5. St Anthony's Church, Scotland Road
6. The Eucharistic elements - bread and wine
7. Icon of Our Lady
8. The Metropolitan (Roman Catholic) Cathedral
9. St George's Greek Orthodox Church, Berkeley Street

PANEL I Jewish Community

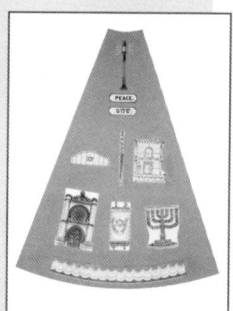

1. PEACE (SHALOM) - central community value
2. Yad - pointer used when reading the Sefer Torah scroll
3. Star of David on entrance to Harold House Jewish Community and Youth Centre, Childwall
4. Rabbi's House next door to former Hope Place Synagogue (now the Unity Theatre)
5. Central front elevation of Liverpool Old Hebrew Congregation Synagogue, Princes Road
6. Sefer Torah scroll with ornate covering
7. Menorah: traditional symbol of the Jewish community and faith

PANEL V Muslim Community

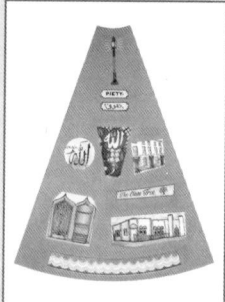

1. PIETY (TAQWA) - central community value
2. 'Allah' in colour with rose flower
3. 'Allah the All Glorious' above the Liver building
4. Brougham Terrace - site of the UK's first Mosque established by Abdulla Quilliam in 1889
5. 'The Olive Tree': the Islamic Resource Centre and shop on Renshaw Street
6. The Mihrab (niche to mark the direction of Mecca and hence prayer) in the Ar Rahma Mosque
7. Front of the Ar Rahma Mosque, Mulgrave Street

PANEL E Sikh Community

1. FELLOWSHIP (SANJIVAL) - central community value
2. Sat Siri Akal = God is Truth
3. Satnah Waheguru = God's name is Truth
4. Ek on Kar SatGuru = God is One by the Grace of God
5. Berkeley Street where the fist Sikh families in Liverpool met for worship
6. United Sikh Association, Community Centre and Gurdwara, Wellington Road
7. Khanda: the Sikh symbol with two crossed swords symbolising the unity of the spiritual and the temporal realms; the central sword representing the Almighty Creator and the circle representing the Oneness and Eternity of God
8. Ek Onkar - God is One
9. Guru Nanak, the founder of the Sikh faith

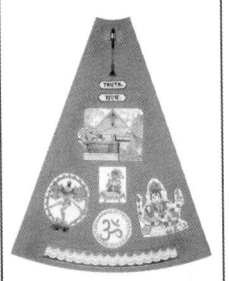

PANEL R Hindu Community

1. TRUTH(FULNESS) (SATYA) - central community value
2. Hindu Cultural Centre, Edge Lane
3. Happy Hindu Goddess on Lotus leaf seat
4. Shiva as Nataraj - Lord of the Dance
5. Ganesha - the deity who removes all obstacles
6. Om -the most powerful sacred syllable and symbol representing the Ultimate Reality and the ultimate creative sound and power that sustains all creation

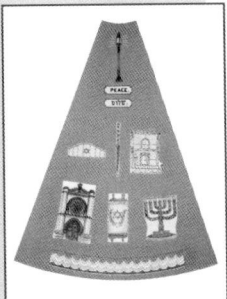

PANEL P Buddhist Community

1. MINDFULNESS - central community value
2. Yama, the Lord of Death who holds the wheel of life and represents impermanence.
3. Traditional Tibetan pattern
4. Tibetan pattern depicting mountains with Mt. Kailash in the middle
5. Entrance and porch of the Duldzin Buddhist Centre, Sefton Park (with Dharma wheel)
6. Dharma wheel Mandala with eight petals/spokes representing the teaching of the Buddha
7. Representation of Buddha Shakyamuni in meditation
8. Tibetan representation of a snow lion - representing a balanced, cheerful mind, free of doubt

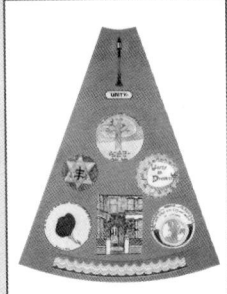

PANEL O Baha'i Community

1. UNITY - central community value
2. Quotes from Abdu'l Baha, (the son and successor of Baha' u'llah) who visited Liverpool
3. The Ring Stone or Greatest Name Symbol
4. Unity in Diversity - a central message of the Baha'i faith
5. Quote from Baha' u'llah, the great Messenger of the Baha'i faith
6. Liverpool Baha'i Centre, Langdale Road
7. Quote from Abdu'l Baha, (the son and successor of Baha' u'llah)

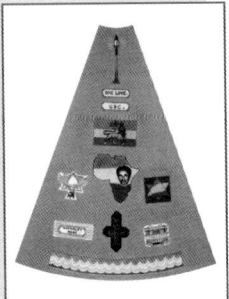

PANEL O Rastafarian Community

1. ONE LOVE ('waddada' in Amharic) - central community value
2. Royal flag of Ethiopia with Lion of Judah
3. Map of Africa with red gold and green and image of the Emperor Haile Selassie
4. Star of David with traditional Rastafarian hand sign
5. Star of David with red, gold and green
6. Waverley Road sign: this was where the Crown Prince Asfa Wossen (later Emperor Amha Selassie 1) lived whilst studying at Liverpool University
7. Ethiopian Orthodox Church Cross
8. Adelphi Hotel, where Emperor Haile Selassie stayed during his visits to Liverpool

PANEL L Christian Community 2

1. LOVE - central community value
2. Crucifix - Christ crucified - the heart of the Christian Faith
3. St Agnes Church, Ullet Road
4. Our Lady and Nicholas: Parish Church of Liverpool
5. 'Thy Word is Truth' - banner from Bridge Chapel, Garston
6. Icon of Our Lady
7. 'How Good is the God we Adore': banner from Bridge Chapel, Garston
8. Liverpool Anglican Cathedral

Central boss: Black Liverbird in Ebony inlay. Design adapted from Rowse's designs for the first Mersey Tunnel in the early 1930s. The Black Liverbird symbolises (together with red gold and green) - the Black African heritage and roots of Liverpool (Europe's oldest Black community and the origins of the City's wealth in the Slave trade) and also, the spiritual symbolism of black as the great well of potential from which emerges all colours and creativity. The Shepherd's crook is a faith symbol representing God as the shepherd of humanity.

Appendix

Liverpool's Zoroastrian/Parsee community heritage

Zoroastrianism: is the oldest revealed, monotheistic world religion, rooted in the teachings of the prophet Zarathustra (Zoroaster) who lived in Persia in the 7th century BC. Zoroastrians believe in One God, **Ahura Mazda** ('Wise Lord'), free-will (humans being subject to the temptations of the destructive spirit *Angra Mainyu*), Judgement, Heaven and Hell and angels. Contrary to popular misconceptions, Zoroastrians do not worship fire, but rather venerate it as a manifestation of Divine qualities. Traditionally, corpses are left exposed in special towers for consumption by vultures so as to avoid polluting the earth (cremation is practised where this is not possible). Zoroastrians place great emphasis upon leading an industrious, honest and charitable life and pioneered the education of women despite opposition from traditionalist Muslim, Hindu and Christian societies.

Following the arrival of Islam in Persia with the Arabs in the 7th century BC, Zoroastrians have fled from persecution and discrimination. Many settled in Bombay and became known as Parsees (because of their Persian heritage).

There is only one Parsee family living in the Liverpool area. However, Liverpool has an important Parsee heritage. It was the city in which the Parsee K.J. Cama established the first Asian firm in Britain: Cama and Co. in the 1850s.

The famous Parsee **Dadabhai Naoroji** also came to Liverpool (and later London) to work in the company. Dadabhai Naoroji helped directly guide and inspire Mahatma Ghandi in the struggle for Indian rights and independence and, following the Parsee teachings on the equality of the sexes, he established the first foundation for female education in India in 1849. Dadabhai became Britain's first Asian MP (elected Liberal MP for Finsbury in 1892).

The Zoroastrian daily prayer *Ashem Vohu* provides a fitting conclusion to our brief guide to some of Liverpool's faith community heritage:

Righteousness (ashoi) is not only good but it is the highest blessing which Thou, Ahura Mazda, hast bestowed upon man. The supreme bliss which lies in righteousness comes to them who practise it for its own sake, that is, for the pure love of it, without thought of fear or favour, or of punishment or reward.